DORLING KINDERSLEY EYEWITNESS BOOKS

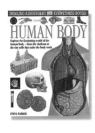 HUMAN BODY
 HURRICANE & TORNADO
 INSECT
 INVENTION
JUNGLE
KNIGHT
 LIFE

 LIGHT
 MAMMAL
 MATTER
 MEDIA & COMMUNICATION
 MEDICINE
 MEDIEVAL LIFE
 MONEY

 MUMMY
 MUSIC
 MYTHOLOGY
 NORTH AMERICAN INDIAN
 OCEAN
 OLYMPICS
 PIRATE

 PLANT
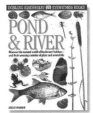 POND & RIVER
 PREHISTORIC LIFE
 PYRAMID
 RELIGION
 REPTILE
 RESCUE

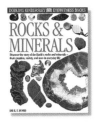 ROCKS & MINERALS
 SEASHORE
 SHARK
 SHELL
 SHIPWRECK
 SKELETON
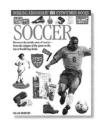 SOCCER

 SPACE EXPLORATION
 SPORTS
 SPY
 TECHNOLOGY
 TIME & SPACE
 TITANIC
 TRAIN

 TREE
 VIKING
 VOLCANO & EARTHQUAKE
 WEATHER
 WHALE
 WILD WEST
 WITCHES & MAGIC-MAKERS

 WORLD WAR I
 WORLD WAR II

DORLING KINDERSLEY EYEWITNESS BOOKS

CAT

Jaguar

Serval

Plaque
showing a
crowned lion,
Limoges, France,
12th century

Tabby cat

Tigers

Inlaid earthenware tile A.D. 1870. The lion is the symbol of St. Mark the evangelist

Abyssinian kittens

DK EYEWITNESS BOOKS

CAT

Written by
JULIET CLUTTON-BROCK

Ocelot

Abyssinian

Maine coon

Ginger and white cat

Black leopard

Puma cub

DK
Dorling Kindersley

Ginger cat

Black and white cat

Bobcat

Early Greek gold
necklace plate

Lion

Puma

DK

Dorling Kindersley
LONDON, NEW YORK, AUCKLAND, DELHI, JOHANNESBURG, MUNICH, PARIS and SYDNEY

For a full catalog, visit

 www.dk.com

Project editor Gillian Denton
Art editor Thomas Keenes
Senior editor Helen Parker
Senior art editor Julia Harris
Production Louise Barratt
Picture research Diana Morris
Special photography Dave King
Additional special photography Philip Dowell
and Colin Keates ABIPP

This Eyewitness ® Book has been conceived by
Dorling Kindersley Limited and Editions Gallimard

© 1991 Dorling Kindersley Limited
This edition © 2000 Dorling Kindersley Limited
First American edition, 1991

Published in the United States by
Dorling Kindersley Publishing, Inc.
95 Madison Avenue
New York, NY 10016
2 4 6 8 10 9 7 5 3

Dorling Kindersley books are available at special discounts for
bulk purchases for sales promotions or premiums. Special
editions, including personalized covers, excerpts of existing
guides, and corporate imprints can be created in large quantities
for specific needs. For more information, contact Special Markets
Dept., Dorling Kindersley Publishing, Inc., 95 Madison Ave.,
New York, NY 10016; Fax: (800) 600-9098

Library of Congress Cataloging-in-Publication Data
Clutton-Brock, Juliet.
Cat / written by Juliet Clutton-Brock;
photographs by Dave King.
p. cm — (Eyewitness Books)
Includes index.
Summary: Text and photographs present the anatomy,
behavior, habitats, and other aspects of wild and domestic cats.
1. Felidae — Juvenile literature. 2. Cats — Juvenile literature.
[1. Felidae. 2. Cats.] I. King, Dave, ill. II. Title.
QL737.C23C58   2000   599.74'428 — dc20 91-9399
ISBN 0-7894-5753-9 (pb)
ISBN 0-7894-5752-0 (hc)

Color reproduction by Colourscan, Singapore
Printed in China by Toppan Printing Co. (Shenzhen) Ltd.

Contents

Leopard

6
What is a cat?
8
The first cats
10
Cat clans
12
The bare bones
14
Inside out
16
Supersenses
18
Magnificent movers
20
Cleaning up
22
Playing cat and mouse
24
The young ones
26
Cat characteristics
28
Top cat
30
Tiger, tiger, burning bright
32
Tree climber
34
Water cat
36
High society
38
Plains drifters

40
Forest felines
42
Speed king
44
Cats' kin
46
The taming of the cat
48
Myths and legends
50
Aristocats
52
Shorthairs
56
Longhairs
58
Curious cats
60
Street life
62
Caring for your cat
64
Index

What is a cat?

CATS ARE POSSIBLY THE MOST BEAUTIFUL and graceful of all animals. They are sleek, with fine fur that is often strikingly marked with spots or stripes (pp. 14–15), and elegant heads with pointed ears and large eyes. Both the wild cat and the domestic cat belong to one family, the Felidae. Although they vary in size from the common house cat to the huge Siberian tiger, they look alike and behave in similar ways; a tiger rolling in the grass looks a lot like a giant tabby (pp. 26–27). Cats have all the features typical of mammals: they walk upright and are warm-blooded, and they have a protective skeleton, a four-chambered heart, and mammary glands which secrete milk to feed the young. Cats are among the most successful of all carnivores, or meat eaters, and most of them live and hunt on their own. This solitary life is possible because cats prey upon animals that are smaller than themselves and are therefore not too difficult to kill. The exception is the lion (pp. 28–29), which hunts in a family group, or pride. The domestic cat is one of the most popular of all animal companions because it is affectionate, intelligent, and playful.

NOW YOU SEE ME...
This jaguar is well-hidden. The striped and spotted fur of the cat family provides very effective camouflage in the great variety of habitats in which cats live. Both stripes and spots blend in well in forests, jungles, grasslands, and plains.

ACCORDING TO THE GOSPEL
The beautiful Lindisfarne Gospels were written and decorated in Saxon Northumbria in Britain, around A.D. 700. The domestic cat was clearly a familiar sight around the countryside at this time.

ADAPT AND SURVIVE
Domestic cats are very adaptable. They can live in a room, a barn, or a palace, and they are found all over the world from tropical Africa to lands of snow and ice, such as Greenland. The cheetah can be successfully tamed, but the domestic cat is the only member of the cat family that lives and breeds happily within human society.

The narrow stripes and tabby markings of this domestic cat are inherited from its wild ancestor

Whiskers are organs of touch and help all cats - big, small, wild, or domestic - to feel objects in the dark

JAPANESE CAPRICE
In certain religions, such as Islam and Buddhism, cats have had a far happier history than in Christianity. The Japanese have a definite sympathy with the mysterious cat, and have often indicated its changeable nature by portraying one cat made up of many.

The mane of the adult male lion is the only obvious sign of sexual difference in the whole cat family

COOPERATIVE CAT
The lion is the only social cat. It lives in a shared territory with other members of its pride and hunts on a cooperative basis. This enables it to hunt herd animals bigger than itself, like antelope and zebra. Like all cats, lions kill their prey by stalking and then leaping on it and biting into the neck (pp. 28–29).

All cats have claws, and all except the cheetah sheath them when at rest (pp. 42–43)

THE CAT THAT WALKED BY HIMSELF
The British writer Rudyard Kipling explained the cat's place in human affection and its need for solitude in a wonderful story called *The Cat That Walked By Himself*.

The first cats

MILLIONS OF YEARS AGO, many cat-like animals walked the earth, some more massive and fierce than any alive today. The earliest fossil ancestors of the cat family come from the Eocene period, some 50 million years ago. These ancestors evolved into the species of large and small cats that are living today, such as the lion and the house cat. Another line of evolution produced the now extinct saber-toothed cats, so-called because the huge canine teeth in the upper jaw were like daggers, or sabers, and the cats killed their prey by stabbing it with these weapon-like teeth. Some saber-toothed cats were large; others were small. The American species *Smilodon*, well-known from the La Brea tar pits in California, was a little larger than a modern tiger.

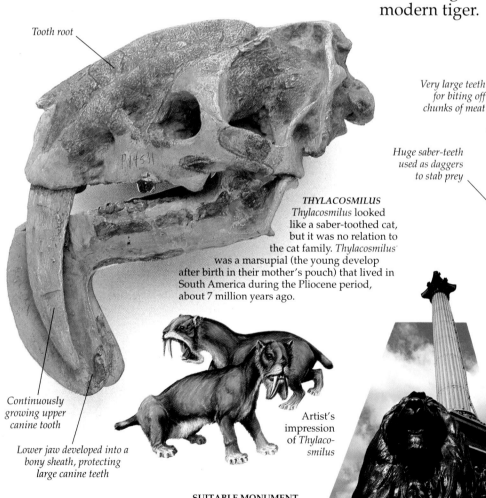

STUCK ON YOU
In the Ice Age, a natural eruption of black, sticky tar at Rancho La Brea, now part of Los Angeles, California, trapped thousands of different animals, including 2,000 saber-toothed *Smilodon*. These carnivores probably got stuck when they rushed into the tar after prey that was trying to escape from them.

Tooth root

Very large teeth for biting off chunks of meat

Huge saber-teeth used as daggers to stab prey

THYLACOSMILUS
Thylacosmilus looked like a saber-toothed cat, but it was no relation to the cat family. *Thylacosmilus* was a marsupial (the young develop after birth in their mother's pouch) that lived in South America during the Pliocene period, about 7 million years ago.

Continuously growing upper canine tooth

Lower jaw developed into a bony sheath, protecting large canine teeth

Artist's impression of Thylaco-smilus

SUITABLE MONUMENT
Sir Edwin Landseer (1802–1873) sculpted the lions that flank Admiral Lord Nelson's column in London's Trafalgar Square, to commemorate British victories in battle. During the last Ice Age, real lions roamed the freezing landscapes of Britain in search of prey like bison and wild horses. The bones of these extinct lions have been found right underneath the Landseer lions in the heart of modern London.

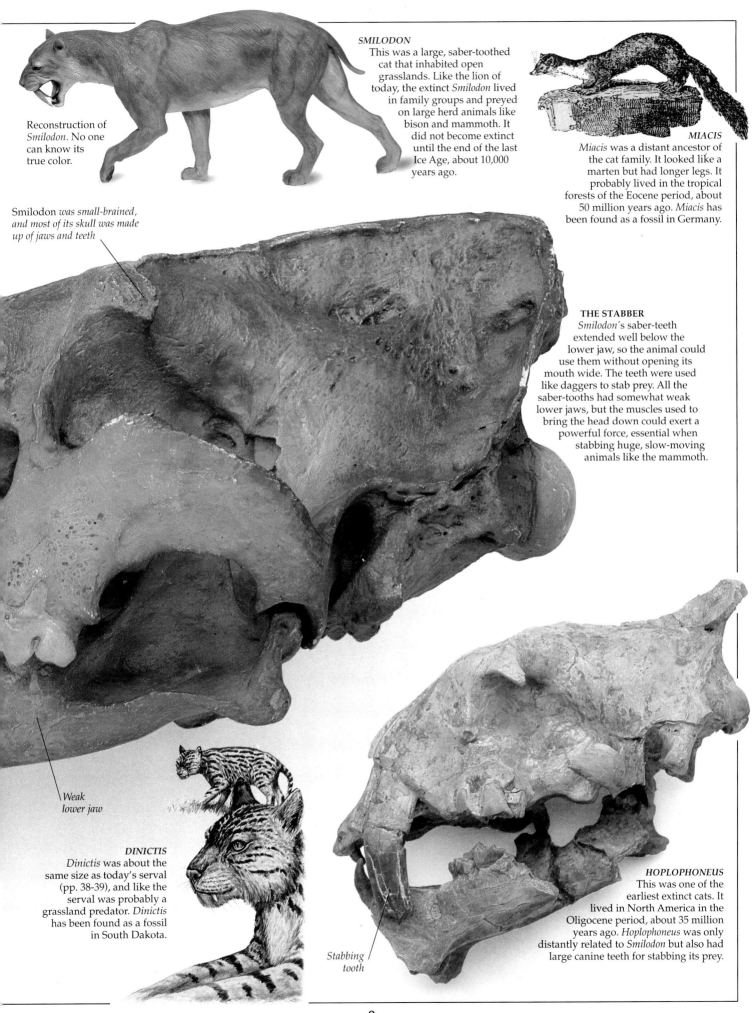

SMILODON

This was a large, saber-toothed cat that inhabited open grasslands. Like the lion of today, the extinct *Smilodon* lived in family groups and preyed on large herd animals like bison and mammoth. It did not become extinct until the end of the last Ice Age, about 10,000 years ago.

Reconstruction of *Smilodon*. No one can know its true color.

MIACIS

Miacis was a distant ancestor of the cat family. It looked like a marten but had longer legs. It probably lived in the tropical forests of the Eocene period, about 50 million years ago. *Miacis* has been found as a fossil in Germany.

Smilodon *was small-brained, and most of its skull was made up of jaws and teeth*

THE STABBER

Smilodon's saber-teeth extended well below the lower jaw, so the animal could use them without opening its mouth wide. The teeth were used like daggers to stab prey. All the saber-tooths had somewhat weak lower jaws, but the muscles used to bring the head down could exert a powerful force, essential when stabbing huge, slow-moving animals like the mammoth.

Weak lower jaw

DINICTIS

Dinictis was about the same size as today's serval (pp. 38-39), and like the serval was probably a grassland predator. *Dinictis* has been found as a fossil in South Dakota.

Stabbing tooth

HOPLOPHONEUS

This was one of the earliest extinct cats. It lived in North America in the Oligocene period, about 35 million years ago. *Hoplophoneus* was only distantly related to *Smilodon* but also had large canine teeth for stabbing its prey.

Cat clans

Cats kill other animals for food, which means that they are part of the order Carnivora (meat eaters) along with about 200 other species, including bears, pandas, dogs, hyenas, raccoons, and weasels. There are four groups within the cat family: the small cats, which includes 28 different species including domestic cats and cats as diverse as the small black-footed cat and the large puma; the large cats (the lion, tiger, jaguar, leopard, and snow leopard); and two groups consisting of only one cat each, the cheetah and the clouded leopard. Wild cats are native to every continent except Australia, where they have been introduced by humans, and Antartica. The domestic cat is descended from one species of small wildcat, *Felis silvestris*, which is still found today in parts of Europe, western Asia, and Africa. The small cats differ from the large cats not only because they are smaller but also because they are unable to roar. Cats have remarkably well-developed senses, fast movements, and very sharp teeth, and are the most highly specialized meat eaters of all the carnivores.

ORIGIN OF THE SPECIES
Carl von Linné (Linnaeus; 1707-1778) was a Swedish botanist. He invented the system of giving Latin names to plants and animals. He called the domestic cat *Felis catus* and the lion *Felis leo*.

PUMA
The puma, or cougar, is an oversized small cat that can purr like a tabby. It lives in North and South America. The first European settlers thought it was a lion but couldn't understand what had happened to its mane!

BOBCAT
This inhabitant of North America looks like a lynx without the long ear tufts. It is the most common wild cat in North America but is seldom seen.

DOMESTIC CAT
Today, there are nearly as many breeds of domestic cats as there are breeds of dogs. They are all descended from the wildcat (*Felis silvestris*).

Small cats

Small cats include all the smaller wild cats as well as the domestic cat. All the small cats live on their own and hunt by night. They are found all over the world in a great variety of habitats, and tragically, many have been hunted almost to extinction for their soft, beautifully patterned fur.

Big cats

The big cats are at the top of the hunting pyramid and require a great deal of meat. They have always been fewer in number than the small cats, which are more easily able to find sufficient food for their needs.

TIGER
The tiger is the largest and heaviest of all the cats. It is a night hunter, preying on animals smaller than itself. Tigers are found from tropical India to icy Siberia.

ON THE SCREEN
The lion has often been used as a symbol of quality. One of the best known advertising cats is the MGM lion, seen here practicing his roar.

Odd cats out

Two members of the cat family are distinct from all others – the clouded leopard and the cheetah. The clouded leopard is a large animal but does not roar like the other big cats, nor does it groom or rest like a small cat. The cheetah is unique because it is a running cat; all others are leaping cats.

CLOUDED LEOPARD
The clouded leopard is about the size of a small leopard but is not closely related. It lives in the forests of Southeast Asia but is rarely seen and is in danger of extinction. Like the true leopard, it often climbs trees.

CHEETAH
The cheetah is unlike all other cats – it does not have sheaths over its claws (pp. 14–15) and it can run at great speed. This ability is an adaptation to life as a hunter on the African grasslands where there are many other competing carnivores.

Ancestors of early cats

Social hunters — Solitary hunters

Leaping cats — Running cats

Other big cats — Clouded leopard — Small cats — Cheetah

Lion

THE DESCENT OF THE CAT
The relationships and fossil history of the different cats are not fully understood. In this diagram, the cheetah is separated from all the others and is called a running cat because it is unique in being able to chase its prey at incredible speed. However, it kills its prey in the same way as all cats – by leaping on it and biting into its neck. All other cats are called leaping cats because they slowly stalk their prey and then leap on it.

The bare bones

THE SKELETON, CONSISTING OF ABOUT 250 BONES, provides a rigid framework for the soft parts of the body, protecting them from shock and injury, and at the same time allowing the cat to move with great agility and suppleness. The skull, in both large and small cats, is highly specialized for killing prey and devouring it in the shortest possible time, before other predators can steal it. The eye sockets (orbits) are large and round to allow a wide field of vision, the hearing parts of the skull are large, and the short jaws open very wide. Cats kill their prey with bites from their very sharp canine teeth and then tear off pieces of meat with their carnassial (tearing) teeth. They do not chew their food, but bolt it down; nor do they gnaw at bones, so they do not need as many teeth as dogs.

NIGHT PROWLER
This snow leopard, hunting at night, reveals its fearsome teeth as it gets ready to attack.

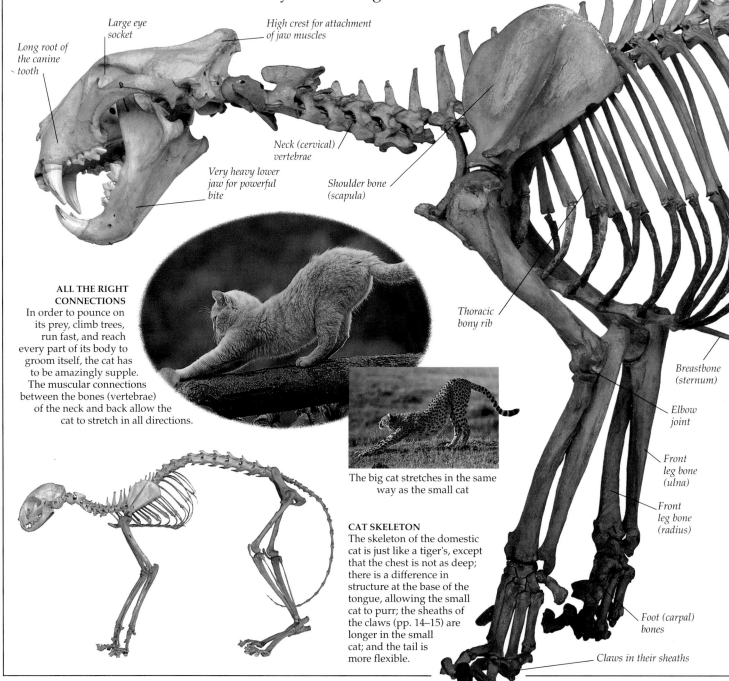

Large eye socket

High crest for attachment of jaw muscles

Long root of the canine tooth

Spine of thoracic vertebrae

Neck (cervical) vertebrae

Very heavy lower jaw for powerful bite

Shoulder bone (scapula)

ALL THE RIGHT CONNECTIONS
In order to pounce on its prey, climb trees, run fast, and reach every part of its body to groom itself, the cat has to be amazingly supple. The muscular connections between the bones (vertebrae) of the neck and back allow the cat to stretch in all directions.

Thoracic bony rib

Breastbone (sternum)

Elbow joint

Front leg bone (ulna)

Front leg bone (radius)

The big cat stretches in the same way as the small cat

CAT SKELETON
The skeleton of the domestic cat is just like a tiger's, except that the chest is not as deep; there is a difference in structure at the base of the tongue, allowing the small cat to purr; the sheaths of the claws (pp. 14–15) are longer in the small cat; and the tail is more flexible.

Foot (carpal) bones

Claws in their sheaths

CAT SKULLS

This skull shows the big, round eye sockets of the domestic cat, its short face, and its large, sharp teeth. In some breeds of domestic cat, like the Persian, the face has been bred to be so short that there is hardly any room for the teeth, and the animal snuffles because it cannot breathe properly through its flattened nose.

Eye socket (orbit)

Biting tooth (incisor)

Killing tooth (canine)

Tearing tooth (carnassial)

Front view of domestic cat skull

Side view of domestic cat skull

Tiger skeleton

Sacral vertebrae

Lumbar vertebrae

Hip bone (pelvis)

Four false ribs, not attached to the sternum

Thigh bone (femur)

Hip joint

Costal cartilages join the ribs to the sternum

Kneecap (patella)

Caudal vertebrae

TIGER SKELETON

The skeletons of all cats are similar. The skull is rounded with short jaws and a largish braincase (cranium). There are seven neck vertebrae, as in most mammals, but they are compressed, making the cat's neck shorter in comparison to the rest of its body. The rib cage is deep and the strong hind leg bones are longer than the foreleg bones. The number of bones in the tail varies from species to species; the tiger, for example, has more bones in its tail than does the bobcat.

Knee joint

Back leg bone (fibula)

Back leg bone (tibia)

JUST A BITE

This lioness can break a bone with one bite of her strong jaws. All cats can open their mouths very wide, owing to the thick bones at the angle of the jaw and the powerful ligaments that join the lower jaw to the upper jaw in a hinge, just below the front of the ear.

The skeleton shows clearly that this Manx cat was completely tailless

MISSING LINK

Although Manx cats did not originate on the Isle of Man in the Irish Sea, they have been known there for over 200 years (pp. 58–59). Their lack of a full tail is thought to be due to inbreeding in the past.

TOEING THE LINE

It is impossible for a person to stand on tiptoe without support; ballet toeshoes have blocks in the toes. The joints and bones of all cats' feet have evolved in such a way that they always walk on their toes.

Heel bone (calcaneum)

Hind foot bones (metatarsals)

Inside out

EVERYTHING ABOUT THE CAT has evolved so that it can feed on other live animals. It has to be a fast thinker, a fast killer, and, in order to outwit other predators, a fast eater. Therefore, all cats are agile and have very fast reactions, and their bodies are thin and powerful. Cats are very intelligent, and their brains are large in relation to the size of their bodies. Their diet consists of meat alone. After a kill, the wild cat will gorge itself on the flesh of its prey, and then may go for several days digesting this meat, before it hunts again. The rough tongue can scrape flesh from bones as well as draw food into the mouth (pp. 20–21). Cats have sweat glands and reduce excess body heat by sweating. However, their fur covering leaves only the glands on the paw pads and, in some cases, the nose, effective for heat loss. The male cat has large anal glands which produce the pungent smell that makes many people prefer to have their tomcats rendered sterile.

FLEHMEN
The special grimace (flehmen) of this lion shows that he is using the Jacobson's (taste-smell) organ to tell if there is a lioness in heat nearby (pp. 16–17). By lifting his head and curling back his upper lip, the lion is drawing the scent-laden air over the Jacobson's organ in the roof of his mouth.

GENE MACHINE
The curly coat of this rex is an abnormality caused by genetic mutation. Inbreeding reduces gene variability and leads to the appearance of abnormal genes in the offspring.

Fur

A fur coat has many uses. It keeps the cat warm, acts as camouflage, carries the scent of the animal, and acts as an organ of touch by means of the sensitive roots of each hair (pp. 16–17). All wild cats have a two-layered coat: an undercoat of fine soft wool, and an outer coat of coarser, longer hairs (guard hairs). The hairs of the outer coat carry the fur's spotted or striped pattern.

Rounded head with short face

Lithe body

Whiskers

Long legs

SPOT ME
The spotted coat of the leopard is perfect for camouflage and makes the cat invisible in the sun-dappled, wooded grasslands where it lives. Only the tawny-yellow eyes of this leopard would be seen, as the cat waits staring intently for any movement that might mean the possibility of a meal.

FUR COATS
It is easy to see how different the furs of cats are when they are placed side by side in this way. It is also easy to see why, for hundreds of years, cat fur has been used to make coats for humans. Today, many people feel that it is cruel to kill animals for their fur.

Tiger

Leopard

Panther

Jaguar

Ocelot

Serval

Claws

Claws are formed of keratin, a protein which also forms the outer layer of skin and is found in human nails. The cat's hind paws have four claws each; the forepaws, five each. The fifth claw is placed like a thumb and helps the cat to grip when climbing or holding prey.

Relaxed

Tightened

CLAWS FOR CONCERN
All cats except the cheetah (pp. 42–43) have a unique arrangement for the protection of their claws. When the claws are relaxed, they are covered by a bony sheath – an extension of the last bone of each toe (top). The claws are rapidly extended by special flexor muscles, and the toes spread out at the same time (above).

NAUGHTY PUSS
This advertisement illustration shows the use – or misuse – of the claws. A cat playing can inflict painful scratches.

PURRFECT COMMUNICATION
The purr is another characteristic of the small cat. In all small cats, the set of bones at the base of the tongue is hard and bony. In big cats, which can only roar (pp. 10–11), these bones are made partly of cartilage. The cat purrs when vibrations are set up in the bones by the nervous system. Both wild and domesticated cats purr when they are content, and female cats purr when suckling their kittens. Cats also purr when they are worried or sometimes when in pain.

Stomach   Kidney   Large intestine

Trachea

Esophagus

Heart

Artery

Vein   Liver   Small intestine

Anus

Bladder

CUT-THROUGH CAT
This picture shows how the digestive system fits into the body cavity and is enclosed by the ribs and the muscles of the belly. The throat leads into the esophagus, which takes the food to the stomach and then to the small intestine. Here the nutritious parts of the food are absorbed into the bloodstream. The waste matter passes through the large intestine and out of the anus.

Long tail for balance

GOOD POINTS
The muscular body of the lioness follows the line of her skeleton. She has a rounded head, a short face, a lithe body, long legs, and a long tail which helps the heavy cat to balance when she leaps on her prey. Sensitive whiskers on the sides of her face help her to find her way in the dark. The parts of the brain that control the senses of sight, smell, hearing, and balance are particularly well-developed in cats.

MUSCLE BOUND
When the skin is removed, the arrangement of the muscles can be seen. The muscles of the shoulder are very powerful and are used when the cat leaps onto its prey.

Supersenses

MOST WILD CATS LIVE on their own and hunt for food at night. Their senses are highly developed and they can move quietly, see everything around them, hear the slightest noise, and smell other animals that are nearby in the dark. The small cat kills quickly and usually eats as fast as possible, because it must always be on the alert, prepared to race up a tree or dive down a hole if danger threatens. Cats have one sense that humans do not have—the "taste-smell" sense—which, among other things, enables the male to know when the female is in heat (pp. 14–15). The homing instinct of cats is legendary and there are countless stories of cats finding their way home over long distances. This may be due partly to their highly developed senses, but they may have other ways of knowing where they are that we do not fully understand. One theory is that they use a strong magnetic sense.

TIME FOR A DRINK
A puma drinks from a freshwater pool. All cats except the sand cat (pp. 38–39) need water regularly.

WATCH THE GAP
Cats are able to judge distances and spaces very accurately. The whiskers and guard (outer) hairs are highly sensitive to the slightest pressure. So if there is room for the fur, there is room for the cat inside.

Pupils expanded *(above)*, narrowed *(below)*

THE EYES HAVE IT
A cat can see about six times better than a human at night because its eyes have a layer of extra reflecting cells (the *tapetum lucidum*) which absorb light. These reflectors shine in the dark when a cat's eyes are caught in the glare of a headlight.

PUPIL POWER
The eyes of a cat are large in relation to its face. They are round and can look forward as well as in a wide angle all around the head. In darkness, the pupils expand to an enormous size in order to allow as much light as possible to enter. In bright light, they narrow to tiny slits in the small cats and to tighter circles in most of the big cats.

CELL MATES
In 1601, the Earl of Southampton was imprisoned in the Tower of London for his part in a rebellion against Queen Elizabeth I. The story goes that his cat, living in the earl's London house, found its way across the city to the Tower. Once there, it crossed roofs and battlements until it found the room in which the earl was imprisoned. But how to get in? The clever cat somehow located the chamber's chimney and climbed down to join its master. This triumphant tale of feline navigational skills may well be true, because this painting was done at the time.

STRETCH 'N' SNIFF
When cats are presented with food or come across any strange object, they are always cautious. They may first reach out and gently tap it with a paw before stretching out and exploring further with the nose.

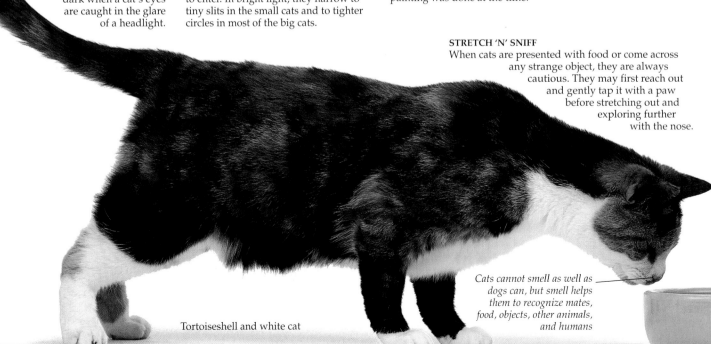

Cats cannot smell as well as dogs can, but smell helps them to recognize mates, food, objects, other animals, and humans

Tortoiseshell and white cat

FIVE SENSES

In all cats, the five senses of sight, hearing, smell, taste, and touch are more highly developed than they are in humans. Although humans are more sensitive to color, cats make better use of the light. When it is too dark for even a cat to see, it can still hear prey or danger and successfully feel its way around with its whiskers, its feet, and the very sensitive outer hairs of its body and tail fur.

Large, funnel-shaped ears draw sound waves into the inner ear so that the cat can judge the direction of a noise

Eyes open wide when a cat is alert and interested. Eyes close to a slit when it is angry or frightened.

THE CAT'S WHISKERS
Whiskers are long, stiff hairs with sensitive nerve endings at their roots. They spread out around the cat's face so that the cat can feel where it is in relation to objects nearby. In bad light, they act as a backup to the cat's sight.

The nose, which has no fur covering, is a very sensitive organ. It draws in scents onto receptors on many thin, curled bones in the front of the skull.

Rough tongue used for grooming the coat, cleaning kittens, and lapping up liquids. Sense of taste is important, because as the cat bolts down its meat, it must be able to distinguish quickly any part that might be rotten and harmful.

Sorrel
Abyssinian

Magnificent movers

EVERY PART OF THE CAT'S BODY is adapted for instant action and perfectly balanced movement. All cats – even the heaviest, like the lion and the tiger – are extremely agile and can leap with great power, although they cannot run very fast over any distance. Their agility and strength is essential, because all cats kill their prey by stalking and then pouncing onto the animal's back and biting its neck. The muscles and bones of the chest and neck are particularly powerful (pp. 14–15), and the ligaments very flexible. Unlike many other carnivores, the cat has collarbones, which prevent it from jarring its shoulders when it leaps from a height. The shoulder blades are placed well on the side of the deep chest (pp. 12–13), which helps the cat to climb, and most of the weight is carried on the forelimbs. Cats that climb trees, like the leopard (pp. 32–33), have long tails, which help them to balance. All cats walk on their toes (pp. 12–13) and their feet have thick, soft pads so they can move quietly.

LUNGING LEO
A big cat is so powerful that it can kill with one lunge of a paw. This lion knows its strength and would usually never hurt another member of its pride.

Cat is at full stretch in mid-leap

Cat puts all four paws together for maximum power at take-off

ONE GIANT LEAP...
All cats can jump, and like other animals they do this by flexing and relaxing the muscles of the limbs and the back, while at the same time balancing with the tail. The cat differs from other jumping animals in that it is able to pinpoint its landing position with great accuracy. This is a necessity for a hunter of small, fast-moving prey.

Cat balances on back paws as it begins leap

Puma cub

NINE LIVES
When cats fall from great heights, they almost always land on their feet. Many of the small cats, as well as the leopard, spend a great part of their lives in trees. Their marvelous sense of balance is an adaptation to the difficult task of hunting a fast-moving animal, such as a squirrel or a bird, while creeping along a flimsy branch. The nervous system has evolved so that the cat, even in the midst of a fall, can right itself so as not to damage its head or the soft parts of its body when it reaches ground. There is a lot of truth in the old saying that "a cat has nine lives" because, by its fast reactions, it can escape from situations that would kill other animals.

When walking or running, diagonal legs go together. Right front leg and left hind leg move in unison.

PRACTICE MAKES PERFECT
All cubs and kittens have to exercise their limbs and muscles before they can achieve the flexibility and agile movements of their parents. This young cub's paws seem too big for its body, but it is practicing running and stalking and will soon be as lithe as its mother.

RUNNING WILD
When a cat runs, it pushes off with both back legs at the same time to achieve maximum forward movement, but places the front paws down separately, although in quick succession. This famous sequence by Eadward Muybridge was taken in 1887, and clearly shows how a cat moves its limbs when running.

Front paws land and cat begins to bring back paws forward

All four paws touch ground

COOL CAT
All cats can probably swim if they have to, but few seem to enjoy it. The tiger is an exception. A good swimmer, it spends a fair amount of time in or near water. Tigers living in the tropical rain forests of Asia use water as a way of keeping cool.

Tail is essential for balance, like the pole carried by a tightrope walker

UP A GUM TREE
All kittens have to learn to climb. At first, just like children, they are frightened of falling and are not good judges of their own capabilities. Kittens often venture too far up a tree or onto a roof and are then terrified of going on or back. After a few misadventures and false starts, however, all but the most timid take the plunge earthward and land on their feet.

Loose skin, and muscles not yet developed

BALANCING ACT
This cat shows how it can walk along the top of a high, narrow fence without concern. It places its paws one in front of the other and is never in danger of falling.

Cleaning up

THE CAT IS AN EXCEPTIONALLY CLEAN ANIMAL. All cats, big, small, wild, and domestic, spend a great deal of time licking their fur with their rough tongues, pulling bits of dirt out of their feet, and wiping their faces with their paws. Grooming spreads the cat's own scent from glands under its skin, over its body and onto objects that it rubs against. Grooming also acts as a method of calming and "relaxing" the cat. It is not known why domestic cats bury their own feces (excreta), but it is a most convenient habit as far as their human owners are concerned. Many wild cats, like the tiger, do not do this, but deposit their excreta in a prominent position to mark their territory with its smell. Although it is the cleanliness itself that seems to us to be all-important to the cat, from the cat's viewpoint, the licking, rubbing, "sharpening of claws," and depositing of excreta in fixed spots (pp. 26–27) is all part of a complex pattern of communication through smell and touch.

Most cats are not fond of water, but these kittens on a beach by famous cat artist Louis Wain (1860–1939) are having a good time

Flexibility of neck allows cat to reach all parts of the body

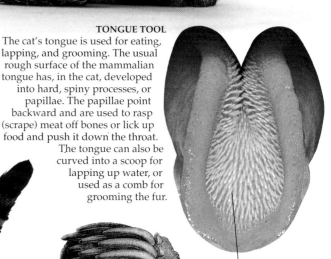

TONGUE TOOL
The cat's tongue is used for eating, lapping, and grooming. The usual rough surface of the mammalian tongue has, in the cat, developed into hard, spiny processes, or papillae. The papillae point backward and are used to rasp (scrape) meat off bones or lick up food and push it down the throat. The tongue can also be curved into a scoop for lapping up water, or used as a comb for grooming the fur.

Papillae, each shaped like a miniature tongue

BELLY BRUSH-UP
By licking its chest and belly, the cat is cleaning its fur and getting it to lie straight and comfortably. This licking also strengthens the cat's own smell after it has been stroked or has fed its kittens.

Close-up of papillae showing how they all point backward

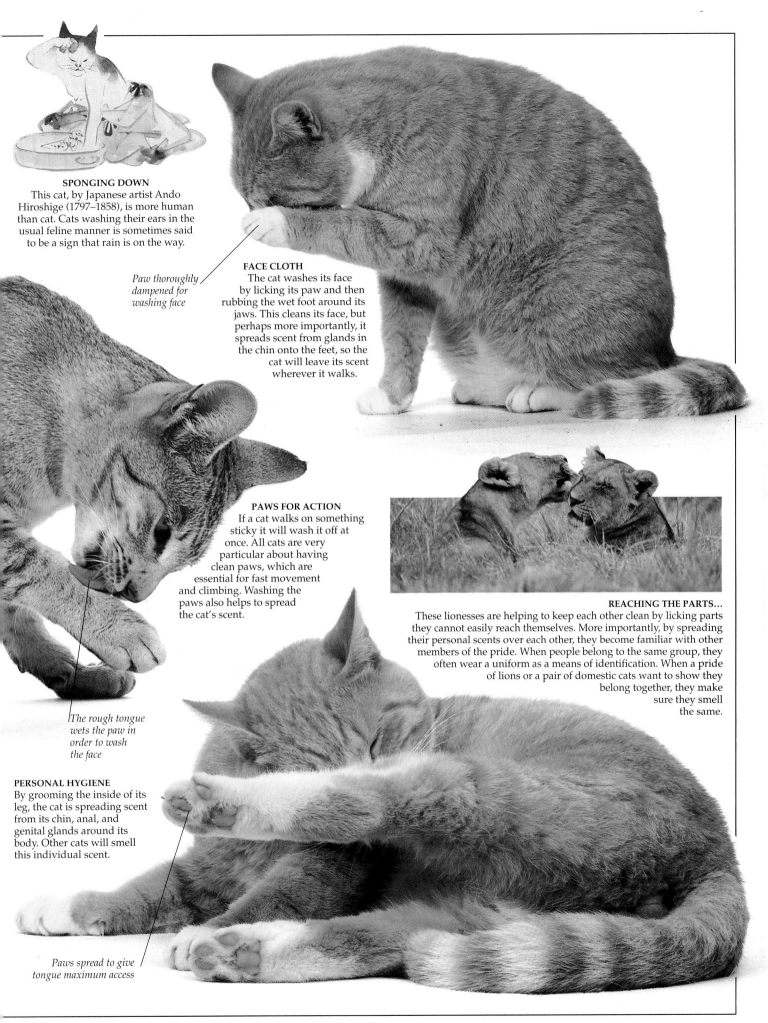

SPONGING DOWN
This cat, by Japanese artist Ando Hiroshige (1797–1858), is more human than cat. Cats washing their ears in the usual feline manner is sometimes said to be a sign that rain is on the way.

Paw thoroughly dampened for washing face

FACE CLOTH
The cat washes its face by licking its paw and then rubbing the wet foot around its jaws. This cleans its face, but perhaps more importantly, it spreads scent from glands in the chin onto the feet, so the cat will leave its scent wherever it walks.

PAWS FOR ACTION
If a cat walks on something sticky it will wash it off at once. All cats are very particular about having clean paws, which are essential for fast movement and climbing. Washing the paws also helps to spread the cat's scent.

REACHING THE PARTS...
These lionesses are helping to keep each other clean by licking parts they cannot easily reach themselves. More importantly, by spreading their personal scents over each other, they become familiar with other members of the pride. When people belong to the same group, they often wear a uniform as a means of identification. When a pride of lions or a pair of domestic cats want to show they belong together, they make sure they smell the same.

The rough tongue wets the paw in order to wash the face

PERSONAL HYGIENE
By grooming the inside of its leg, the cat is spreading scent from its chin, anal, and genital glands around its body. Other cats will smell this individual scent.

Paws spread to give tongue maximum access

Playing cat and mouse

IN THE WILD, all cats feed on the flesh of the animals they have killed. Cats are solitary hunters, except for the lion, which hunts in a family group (pride, pp. 28–29). Cats usually kill animals smaller than themselves, although occasionally they will attack a larger animal. Motionless animals sometimes escape attack, but with practice, cats can recognize prey by sound and scent alone. They have an excellent memory for places and will return many times to a spot where they once had a successful hunt. Cats stalk their prey, sometimes for a long time, then, with a sudden rush, leap on it and sink their sharp canine teeth into the neck. Small cats feed mostly on mice, birds, lizards, beetles, and any other small animal they can catch. Large cats, like the leopard, feed on bigger animals—about the size of a goat—and often drag their prey up into trees to keep it away from other predators.

TOM AND JERRY
In the famous cartoon, quick-witted mouse Jerry often gets the better of the swashbuckling but slightly stupid Tom – not often the case in real life.

A stalking cat holds its body close to the ground

READY FOR ACTION
This black leopard (also known as a panther) is stalking and getting ready for the kill. Every part of the body is alert. A cat on the prowl moves very slowly and silently until it is close enough to make a quick and decisive pounce. All cats hunt in this way, from a lion killing a buffalo to a domestic cat killing a house mouse.

The pads on a cat's paws help it to move silently

MEDIEVAL MOUSERS
This picture comes from a 13th-century book, *The Harleian Bestiary*. Although the cats are not at all realistically painted, it is interesting because it is such an early illustration of cats with a rat.

IN FOR THE KILL
Cats often choose a vantage point from which they can see but not be seen. This cat may have sat absolutely silently and still on the fence for some time, watching the happenings in the grass below, before leaping down with great accuracy on the unsuspecting prey.

Black panther

A FISHY BUSINESS
The fishing cat of India does not hunt for its food quite like any other cat. It can flip fish out of the water with its slightly webbed paws, and has been seen diving for fish and catching them in its mouth.

TELLING TAILS
The cat's tail is an indicator of its moods. It lashes the tail when angry and twitches it gently back and forth when concentrating or contented.

RUNNING DOWN
The cheetah and the springboks are keeping a wary eye on each other. The cheetah will not begin to hunt unless there is an antelope on its own in a vulnerable position. The antelope know this and will not be disturbed unless the cheetah comes too close. However, once the prey has been singled out, the cheetah will pursue it at great speed.

A PRACTICED KILLER
Many cats, both wild and domestic, play with their prey before killing it. Mother cats teach their kittens how to hunt by capturing prey and then releasing it so the kittens can watch their actions. It is not really known why adult cats with no kittens still play with their prey.

A cat playing with a toy is reacting as if it were prey

Serval

BIG MEAL
With its massive teeth, this tiger can snap a bone with one bite and will devour a whole carcass, skin and all.

CHICKEN DINNER
This serval, like other small cats, crouches down to eat its food. When big cats eat, they tend to lie down with the food positioned between their front paws. Small cats begin by eating the head, which is often swallowed whole.

23

The young ones

THE YOUNG OF THE LARGE CATS are usually called cubs, while the young of the small cats are called kittens. All cats, whether large or small, are tiny and helpless when they are born, and are blind until they are at least nine days old. There are usually about four kittens in a litter, and the mother looks after them on her own with no help from the father cat. Cats need a secure place in which to give birth. Domestic cats usually select a safe, dark spot, like a drawer or a cupboard. In the wild, most members of the cat family, from the bobcat to the tiger, give birth in a den. Kittens take around 65 days to gestate (develop) in the mother's womb, and after birth the mother suckles them for six to eight weeks before they are weaned and begin to eat meat. They are fully independent at about six months, but many young cats stay with their mothers for up to two years. The gestation period of cubs, such as the lion cub, is between 100 and 119 days. When they are born, they are very small compared to the size of the mother, and they are not weaned until they are up to six months old.

Leopard with cubs in their den

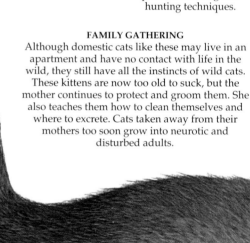

KNITTING KITTEN
The kitten in this Japanese scroll is happily playing with a ball of wool. Toys play an important role - they stand in for prey, allowing kittens to practice catching and hunting techniques.

FAMILY GATHERING
Although domestic cats like these may live in an apartment and have no contact with life in the wild, they still have all the instincts of wild cats. These kittens are now too old to suck, but the mother continues to protect and groom them. She also teaches them how to clean themselves and where to excrete. Cats taken away from their mothers too soon grow into neurotic and disturbed adults.

THE COURT OF THE KING
When a lioness comes into heat and is ready to mate, the chief lion in a pride stays close to her and keeps other lions from approaching. He mates with her many times over the two or three days that she is receptive to him. Each time takes only a few seconds.

Kitten grows adult coat of fine hairs over its woolly undercoat

MOUSERS MATING
A female cat only allows a male to mate with her when she is in heat. With domestic cats, this usually happens twice a year. Each mating takes only a few seconds but may occur several times with different males in the three to five days that the female is in heat (pp. 60–61).

IDENTITY CRISIS
The coats of cubs and kittens are often marked differently than the adults'. This spotted baby is, in fact, a puma. Its spots merge into stripes and it has a ringed tail. The rings and spots slowly fade as the cub grows up. Lion cubs also often have spots, which fade as they mature. In some domestic breeds, such as the Siamese, the kittens are born with a pale coat. The dark points develop as the cat grows.

Sorrel Abyssinian cat and kittens

Mother's rough tongue grooms kitten, helping it to understand about other cats' scents

Legs are slightly bandy and uncertain at first

PLAYING AROUND
Play is an essential part of growing up. It teaches the young animal how to kill its prey and how to "get along" with its fellows. These kittens have to learn how to fight, but they must learn when to stop as well so that they are not badly hurt. Play also exercises the muscles of young animals and helps the brain and nervous system to develop quick reactions.

CUB CARRIAGE
All mother cats are expert at carrying their young from place to place at the first hint of danger. This lioness has grasped the loose skin around the neck of her cub between her teeth and lifts it off the ground without hurting it at all.

Several pairs of teats for suckling – each kitten has its own teat and feeds from no other

Engraving of a terrified cat

Cat characteristics

Cats behave in similar ways, whether large or small, wild or tame. The wild cat gives birth in her den, protected from predators. The house cat, secure in her home, still seeks a safe, dark place to have her young. Apart from the lion, all cats are solitary hunters and eat alone as well. They are strongly territorial animals, and all mark their territory, whether it is the backyard or a stretch of forest, in the same way – by spraying and by depositing excreta. They also exchange scents in the same ways, by rubbing and licking each other. Both large and small cats communicate with one another and make various noises. Yowling and meowing are two sounds familiar to everyone. Cats sleep a great deal, mostly in the day, so that they are ready for the activities of the night. Even domestic cats will follow this pattern of behavior, and do not change their schedule to suit their human owners, except when feeding times are concerned. Unlike dogs, cats can rarely be trained; they have adjusted to living with humans, but have never changed their essential character.

LION LINGO
Ever since the evolution of our human ancestors several million years ago, the roar of the lion has been the most frightening of all animal sounds. However, the lion roars as a means of communicating with the rest of the pride, rather than to frighten its prey.

CAT NAP
Cats sleep a great deal. In some hot countries, they may sleep as much as 18 hours a day, hunting and feeding in the cooler hours. Cats do not usually sleep in long stretches but in a series of short periods. They often have one eye partly open, on the lookout for danger.

FRIEND...
Cats value their personal space. This cat feels hers is threatened and that the other cat has come too close, so she has crouched down low in a defensive position. Sometimes cats raise all their hairs so that they appear enormous.

Flattened ears are a warning sign

Hissing indicates that this cat does not want to be interfered with and will fight if she has to

PUTTING OUR HEADS TOGETHER
Cats that live together, like domestic cats or lions, sometimes rub each other's heads to show that they have no intention of fighting. Young cats do this more often, especially when they are excited.

LEGGINGS
Cats often rub against people's legs. It shows affection and also puts the cat's personal scent on the human.

LEAVING A MESSAGE
All cats mark their territory with urine and secretions from their glands. This is called spraying, and all cats do it in the same way. The cat backs up to a post or tree, lifts its rump high and, with the tail held straight up, discharges a stream of pungent fluid against the object.

SMARTENING UP
Cats spend a good deal of their time "sharpening their claws." What they are really doing is stretching their limbs by digging their claws into a tree (or a sofa!), and pulling the claws downward. The claws are probably not sharpened by this act, but they are cleaned, and the muscles of the feet and limbs are exercised. Sometimes a house-proud cat owner will have the cat's claws removed because it is destroying furniture, but this denies the cat one of its most natural activities.

Back slightly arched to make cat look bigger

LIONESS SCRATCHING
Lions can tear the bark off a tree when "sharpening their claws."

CAT CLUB
This illustration of a cat's club from a 19th-century children's book presents a delightfully fanciful idea of cats socializing and having a good time. In real life, domestic cat colonies are based on the availability of food supplies, and consist of extended families of closely related females, with perhaps a few dominant males attached.

...OR FOE?
Cats test each other's reactions with an explorative paw. This cat is seeing how near he can go to the tortoiseshell cat. Because he is getting a negative reaction he will probably stalk off, pretending to be more interested in something else.

Twitching tail shows that the cat is in an excited state

ROLY-POLY
Both large and small cats roll over on their backs to show affection. They expose their bellies in this way only when they feel totally secure. Rolling is often done by female cats when they are coming into heat (pp. 24–25).

Top cat

MORE THAN 10,000 years ago, when humans hunted animals and gathered roots and berries, there were lions in all of Europe and Asia as well as in Africa. The lions competed with humans for the same prey and gained the respect and fear of their human rivals that exists to the present day. Today, except for a small population in the Gir Forest in northwest India, lions are found only in Africa. They live in family groups, or prides, of up to 12 animals and help each other to hunt. Because they hunt in a group, lions are the only cats that are able to kill animals larger than themselves. The role of the males is to defend the territory. They do this by pacing around it, by roaring, and by marking trees and posts with their urine (pp. 26–27). The females (lionesses) do most of the hunting. Each lioness will give birth to about five cubs every two years. If a new lioness joins a pride, the dominant (lead) male sometimes kills the cubs she already had before he mates with her.

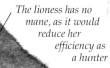

PERSIAN PLATE
This beautiful plate from Iran (formerly Persia) shows a lion standing with the sun rising behind him. This was the symbol of kingship.

THE KING
His magnificent mane, heavy body, and huge canine teeth ensure that the lion rules his world. Although lionesses are the hunters of a pride, the male lions are given prime place at a kill and are allowed to feed first.

African lion and lioness

THE PRIDE
The composition of a pride varies, but females always outnumber males. When young males reach adulthood, they either oust any older lions from the pride or, if unsuccessful, they leave the pride and attach themselves to a group of females. A pride of lions shares its territory with many other meat-eaters, which compete for every scrap of food left over when the pride has had its fill.

MATE TO KING
Lionesses in a pride are usually related as sisters, daughters, and aunts. The lioness has a powerful, lithe body and can creep stealthily up to prey before moving in for the kill.

The lioness has no mane, as it would reduce her efficiency as a hunter

LEO
People born under the astrological sign of Leo are said to be proud, brave, strong, and self-centered — just like the king of beasts himself.

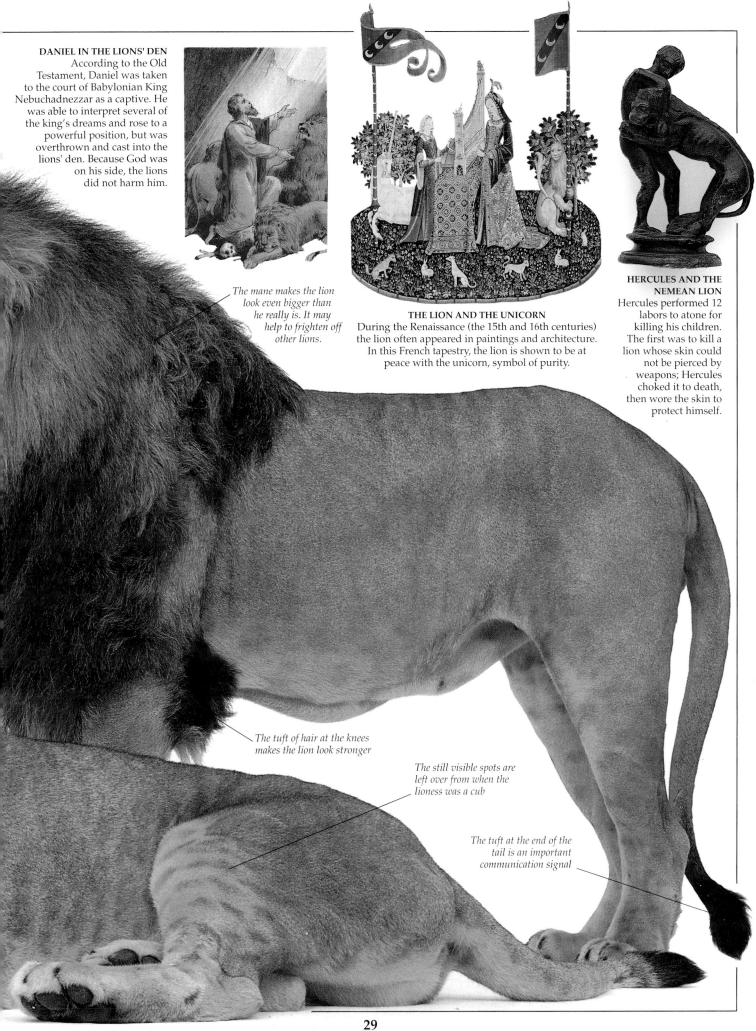

DANIEL IN THE LIONS' DEN
According to the Old Testament, Daniel was taken to the court of Babylonian King Nebuchadnezzar as a captive. He was able to interpret several of the king's dreams and rose to a powerful position, but was overthrown and cast into the lions' den. Because God was on his side, the lions did not harm him.

The mane makes the lion look even bigger than he really is. It may help to frighten off other lions.

THE LION AND THE UNICORN
During the Renaissance (the 15th and 16th centuries) the lion often appeared in paintings and architecture. In this French tapestry, the lion is shown to be at peace with the unicorn, symbol of purity.

HERCULES AND THE NEMEAN LION
Hercules performed 12 labors to atone for killing his children. The first was to kill a lion whose skin could not be pierced by weapons; Hercules choked it to death, then wore the skin to protect himself.

The tuft of hair at the knees makes the lion look stronger

The still visible spots are left over from when the lioness was a cub

The tuft at the end of the tail is an important communication signal

Tiger, tiger, burning bright

Tigers are the biggest and most powerful of all cats. They used to live in small numbers in many of the forests of India, Southeast Asia, and China as far north as Siberia. Today, this magnificent animal is an endangered species, clinging to survival in a few tropical forest reserves, and in swamps such as those of the Ganges River delta in India. The biggest of all tigers come from the snow-covered forests of Siberia, but there are only about 200 still living there in the wild. Their habitat has been gradually destroyed, and they have been hunted for sport almost to the point of extinction. Tigers are solitary hunters of large prey like deer and wild pig, and they defend their territories from all intruders. This means that to survive in any numbers, they need to spread over a very wide area of forest. Like all cats, tigers stalk their prey, but can only run fast for a short time, so they must get close before they can spring for the kill. Tigers spend a good deal of time keeping cool in or near rivers, and they often hide the carcasses of their prey in dense thickets or in water.

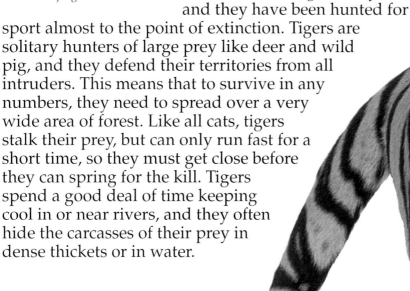

STORM TIGER
In this famous picture, painted by French artist Henri Rousseau (1844–1910), it is hard to see the stalking tiger, camouflaged in a rain-lashed jungle.

NOBLE CAT
The English poet William Blake (1757–1827) wrote in his famous poem *The Tyger*, "What immortal hand or eye could frame thy fearful symmetry?" Indeed, the lion may be called the king of the beasts because of its great mane and proud carriage, but to many people, the tiger looks more awesome. Tigers in India weigh up to 573 lb (260 kg), and the Siberian tiger is even heavier.

The tiger's stripes camouflage it in long grass and forests

Very long, closely striped tail

Heavy body is close to the ground, so the tiger is hidden in grass or water

MASS MURDER
The tiger was respected in India until Europeans settled there in large numbers in the eighteenth century. They considered it a good day's "sport" to slay the tiger from the safety of an elephant's back. In the mid-nineteenth century, when the British ruled India, huge numbers of tigers were slaughtered during shooting parties. In 1888, the British even offered a reward to anyone who killed a tiger. Today, the tiger is again respected, and the Indian government has set up Project Tiger to save it from extinction.

ONE TOO MANY?
A mosaic pavement dating from the first to second century A.D. was discovered in London, England. It shows the Roman god Bacchus, who was the god of wine, nonchalantly riding a tiger.

TIGER BY A TORRENT
This hanging scroll, painted in 1795 by the Japanese artist Kishi Ganku (1756–1838), depicts in great detail a fierce tiger beside a raging torrent.

The stripes on the back are farther apart than those on the legs

Rounded head with long whiskers

Man–eating tigers

Although tigers do not usually kill humans, sometimes they do become "man-eaters." This is either because they are too old or weak to kill wild animals, or because people are fishing or working in their territories and scaring away their natural prey. In India, the government is doing everything it can to keep people and tigers apart.

The huge paw is so powerful that it can knock prey over with one blow

SOLDIER SANDWICH
This large mechanical "toy" was made during the latter part of the Mogul empire (1526–1857) in India. When wound by the handle on the side, the tiger attacks the English soldier.

EYES IN THE BACK OF YOUR HEAD
As tigers almost always attack from behind, forest workers in the Sundarbans forest and swamp between India and Bangladesh have found that a face mask worn on the back of the head has stopped tigers from attacking them.

Tree climber

LEOPARDS LIVE IN WOODED GRASSLANDS in Africa and southern Asia and are the biggest cats to climb trees regularly. They are skilled climbers and can scale a vertical tree trunk with complete ease. They are bulkier than cheetahs, but not as heavy as lions or tigers. They are secretive, stealthy animals and hunt mostly at night, but they are sometimes seen in daylight hours. Leopards usually live on their own. They occasionally prey upon domestic livestock, but they also kill animals such as baboons and cane rats, which destroy crops. Both males and females defend their territory by spray-marking branches and tree trunks and by driving away intruders. Cubs are looked after by the mother until they are about two years old, when they can fend for themselves. Leopards are under threat everywhere, mainly because of the destruction of their habitat, but also because they are hunted for their fur.

LEAFY LARDER
This lounging leopard has clearly had too much to eat. Leopards often carry the animals they kill into trees. This protects the carcasses (dead bodies) from packs of hyenas and jackals, which would soon scrounge the food from the solitary leopard if it were left on the ground.

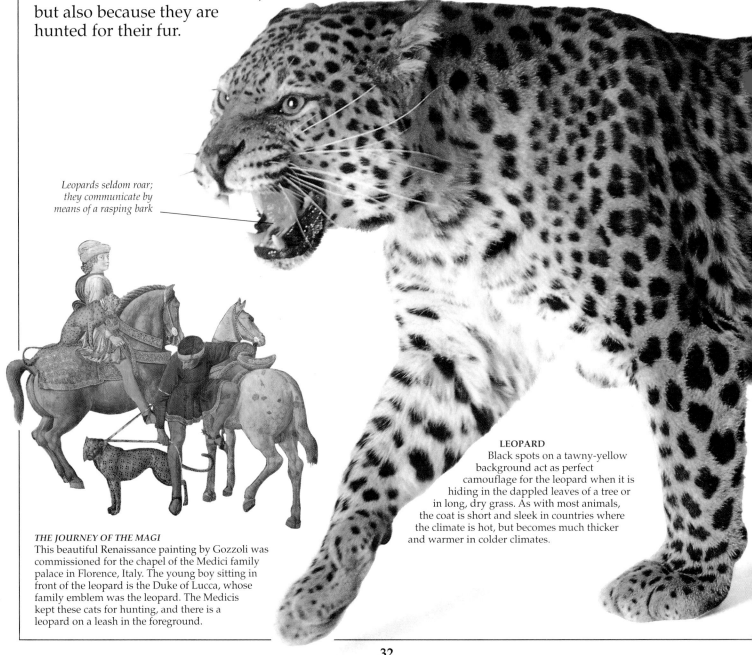

Leopards seldom roar; they communicate by means of a rasping bark

THE JOURNEY OF THE MAGI
This beautiful Renaissance painting by Gozzoli was commissioned for the chapel of the Medici family palace in Florence, Italy. The young boy sitting in front of the leopard is the Duke of Lucca, whose family emblem was the leopard. The Medicis kept these cats for hunting, and there is a leopard on a leash in the foreground.

LEOPARD
Black spots on a tawny-yellow background act as perfect camouflage for the leopard when it is hiding in the dappled leaves of a tree or in long, dry grass. As with most animals, the coat is short and sleek in countries where the climate is hot, but becomes much thicker and warmer in colder climates.

Spotless

The sleek black panther is actually a leopard with hidden spots. The black color comes from a combination of genes that can occur in many other species, including the jaguar and the domestic cat. Panthers behave just like spotted leopards and breed freely with them.

PANTHER
If you look closely you can see the spots on this black panther's coat. This form of leopard coat is most common in the forests of Southeast Asia.

BAGHEERA
Bagheera the black panther played an important part in the upbringing of Mowgli, the jungle boy from Rudyard Kipling's *The Jungle Book*.

SNOW LEOPARD
This very rare, large cat is not the same species as the true leopard. It lives only in the high mountains of central Asia. Snow leopards are solitary hunters and feed on wild goats, deer, and marmots.

The spots look much better on a leopard than on a fur coat

The leopard's tail is long and darkly ringed

The soft–looking paw hides sharp claws used for killing prey and climbing trees

BENIN BRONZE
This bronze plaque, made in the Benin kingdom in Nigeria in the 16th or 17th century, decorated the king's palace. The leopard was an important animal in Benin myths and was known as the King of the Bush. It was chosen as ruler over the animals for its power, beauty, good nature, and wisdom, and only the king was allowed to kill leopards.

Water cat

JAGUAR
This engraving shows clearly what a sturdy cat the jaguar is.

THE JAGUAR IS THE ONLY LARGE CAT to be found on the American continents. The name jaguar comes from *yaguara*, its name in the languages of the Amazon peoples. It lives throughout South America, as far south as Patagonia, and until quite recently, jaguars were also fairly common in the southwestern United States. However, although it is protected today, the jaguar is nevertheless in danger of extinction, because of continued destruction of its forest habitats for development, and because, until recently, thousands were killed for their exceptionally beautiful, spotted coats. The jaguar is similar to the leopard, but larger and less lithe and agile. A solitary hunter, it kills tapirs, sloths, turtles, and other small animals. It can climb trees, but not very well, and prefers to hunt at ground level or in the water. A jaguar maintains a territory that varies from 2 to 200 square miles (5 to 500 square km), depending on the availability of prey.

CAT CULT
The jaguar played an important part in much South American mythology. This pottery vessel from the Inca civilization in Peru shows a jaguar eating its victim.

Long tail, supposedly used as bait for fish

GRUNTER HUNTER
The jaguar is not as bold a hunter as the leopard and is generally slower. Unlike other big cats, it rarely roars. It grunts frequently when hunting and growls when threatened. Jaguars have sometimes been tamed, and occasionally one has even been known to live in a house, like a huge pussycat!

Ringed spots merge to blotches on the belly

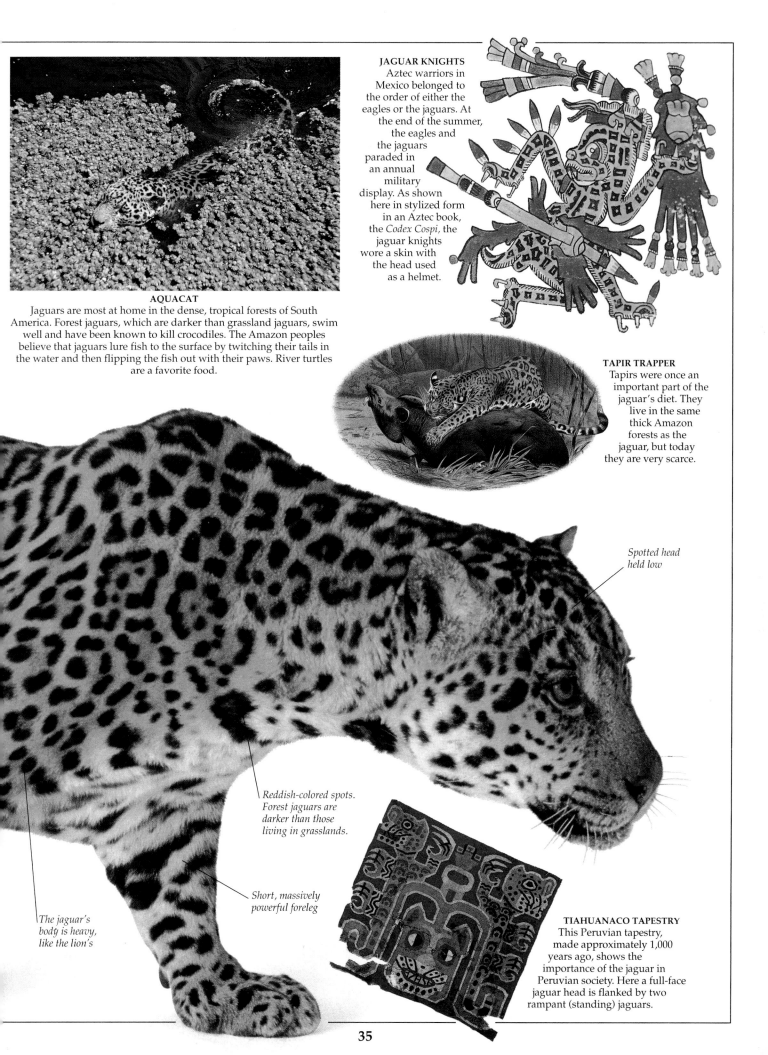

JAGUAR KNIGHTS
Aztec warriors in Mexico belonged to the order of either the eagles or the jaguars. At the end of the summer, the eagles and the jaguars paraded in an annual military display. As shown here in stylized form in an Aztec book, the *Codex Cospi,* the jaguar knights wore a skin with the head used as a helmet.

AQUACAT
Jaguars are most at home in the dense, tropical forests of South America. Forest jaguars, which are darker than grassland jaguars, swim well and have been known to kill crocodiles. The Amazon peoples believe that jaguars lure fish to the surface by twitching their tails in the water and then flipping the fish out with their paws. River turtles are a favorite food.

TAPIR TRAPPER
Tapirs were once an important part of the jaguar's diet. They live in the same thick Amazon forests as the jaguar, but today they are very scarce.

Spotted head held low

Reddish-colored spots. Forest jaguars are darker than those living in grasslands.

Short, massively powerful foreleg

The jaguar's body is heavy, like the lion's

TIAHUANACO TAPESTRY
This Peruvian tapestry, made approximately 1,000 years ago, shows the importance of the jaguar in Peruvian society. Here a full-face jaguar head is flanked by two rampant (standing) jaguars.

High society

THE LYNX, BOBCAT, AND PUMA, or cougar, are called small cats, although they are not particularly small (the puma is actually the largest of all the small cats). However, their body structure is like the small cats and not like the big cats. The lynx and the bobcat are alike, and different from all other cats, in that they have very short tails. Both cats feed on animals the size of hares, and in Canada, lynx numbers vary from year to year, depending on the population of its main prey, the snowshoe hare. The bobcat lives in North America, the lynx in North America, Europe, and Asia, and the puma in North and South America. Although the lynx is found in forests in Europe, all three are most at home among rocky landscapes and high up on mountain slopes, sometimes as much as 15,000 ft (4,500 m) above sea level.

ELIZABETHAN LYNX
A lynx, illustrated 500 years ago in England.

TRAPPED
Hunting for bobcat and lynx is still permitted in North America, and some 70,000 bobcats a year are caught for the fur trade, often in vicious traps like this. Many people believe these traps should be banned as they have been in Britain for a number of years.

A bobcat cleaning itself, by the American artist and naturalist John James Audubon (1785–1851)

Short, stumpy tail

Bobcat

Unlike the lynx, the bobcat has only short tufts on its ears

BOBCAT
The spotted coat of the bobcat camouflages it in the rocks and bushy vegetation where it lives. Bobcats are solitary hunters that prey on small animals. In good weather they will sunbathe in places where they feel secure. When mating, they caterwaul like domestic cats, but their screams are louder and more shrill. The female gives birth in a den lined with grass or moss and hidden in rocks.

Thick side whiskers

Unlike the bobcat and the lynx, the puma has a long, furry tail with a black tip

The hind legs are longer than the front legs, making the puma a good stalker

The puma's coat can vary in color, but the underside is always pale

LYNX

The lynx is best adapted to life in high pine forests and thick scrub where its unspotted, brownish coat is invisible against moss and rocks. The long tufts on its ears are thought to help the lynx to hear well in dense forests where sound does not carry far. It also has very big feet which, in winter, are covered with thick fur that acts like a snowshoe and prevents the lynx from sinking into the snow.

Lynx in summer coat

Lynx in winter coat

PUMA POWER

Around 600 B.C. in the Mochica culture in Peru, the puma was worshipped as a god. This sacred golden puma might have been used for some kind of ritual. It is intricately decorated with rows of double-headed snakes.

PUMA

The puma is an adaptable cat, as much at home on the inhospitable, windswept shores at the tip of South America as on the slopes of the Colorado mountains in the western United States. It hides in rocky places and is a good climber, so it is seldom seen even though it hunts by day as well as by night. Pumas have large territories and cover many square miles in their hunt for prey.

The pupils are circular and do not contract to slits as in most smaller cats

Puma

CHANGE OF SCENE

The puma is often found in mountainous regions, but it also lives in the tropical rainforests of the Amazon.

Plains drifters

MANY CATS LIVE in savannas (grasslands), plains, and deserts. The lion is the largest savanna cat. Two other well-sized plains and savanna cats, the serval and the caracal, are widespread, ranging over the whole African continent and into western Asia. They are considerably bigger than the rest of the plains and savanna cats. Cats from these environments are mainly nocturnal, and hunt for small animals like birds, rodents, lizards, beetles, and snakes. They have longer legs than forest cats and are fairly speedy over short distances, as they have to escape from larger predators, such as hyenas, that might kill them for food. The caracal is also called the desert lynx because it has tufts on its ears like a northern lynx, but its tail is not as short as the lynx's. The serval has been hunted in East Africa for its meat as well as its fur – not for the western fur trade but for traditional cloaks, or *carosses*, worn by East Africans.

Black ears with tufts of hair about 1.75 in (4.5 cm) long

CARACAL
Caracal is a Turkish word meaning "black ears." The caracal has a wider distribution than the serval and is found in western Asia and India, as well as in Africa. It usually has a litter of two or three kittens which are born in borrowed burrows, rock holes, or thick scrub. It does not make many sounds, but has a loud bark which it uses to call its mate.

BIRD BASHER
In India and Persia (now Iran), the caracal, which is easily tamed, was trained to catch rabbits and birds. It is a supreme bird catcher, sometimes leaping up and batting a bird right out of the air. Caracals climb well, and have been known to kill eagles roosting in trees.

Long, strong legs allow bursts of speed

IN UP TO THE NECK
The caracal lives in tall grasslands, dry scrub, and semi-desert.

SERVAL
The serval is one of the most striking of the savanna cats. With its small head, spotted coat, and long legs, it looks like a small cheetah. It lives near water and hunts small animals. Like the caracal, the serval climbs well and catches birds.

SAND CAT
The rarely seen sand cat is a true desert dweller. It sleeps during the sweltering heat of day in a dune burrow or under scrub. At night, it comes out of its den to hunt small desert animals like lizards and mice. It manages to exist without water, getting sufficient liquid from its prey. The sand cat has thick, furry pads on its feet, enabling it to move fast over soft sand, and its yellow-brown coat blends in with the desert. Sand cats live in the Sahara and the deserts of western Asia.

Short, ringed tail with dark tip

Very long front legs built for speed

Short, dense fur keeps the cat warm at night and cool in the day

Tail is one third the length of the head and body

BLACK-FOOTED CAT
This is the smallest of all wild cats, less than half the size of an African wildcat (pp. 44–45), but it is said to be very fierce. So-called because the soles of its feet are black, it lives in open, semi-desert country in southern Africa.

Forest felines

Ocelot

Most small cats live in woodlands, forests, or jungles. Forest cats, like all members of the family Felidae except the lion (pp. 28–29), are solitary hunters that kill smaller animals such as mice and lizards. They feed when they can, and will eat just about anything they are able to catch. Most are very striking in appearance, with powerful, lithe bodies, spotted or striped fur, and huge eyes to help them hunt at night (pp. 16–17). They are extremely shy and hard to see in their habitats, where they are well camouflaged. They are generally silent creatures, but the males try to drive off their enemies by caterwauling. All the species are in danger of extinction both from increasing loss of habitat and also because, in spite of legal protection and a great deal of international publicity, they are still hunted for their fur, particularly in South America.

MARGAYS
The margay looks like a smaller version of the ocelot, but it is slimmer with longer legs and tail. It feeds on birds and lives in forest trees in Central and South America. Very little is known about it.

LEOPARD CAT
The leopard cat is the most common wild cat of southern Asia. It is about the same size as a domestic cat and also looks like one. It is a good climber and an excellent swimmer and has therefore been able to colonize small offshore islands. In China, it is known as the money cat because its spots look like small coins.

NOT A LOTTA OCELOT!
Although mainly a forest cat, the ocelot is also found in grass and scrubland from Arizona to Argentina. Ocelots hunt by day, swim well, and often live in pairs. Forest ocelots have a darker coat than those that live in scrub. In Mexico, because of the stripes around its neck, it is known as *tigrillo* or "little tiger." It is the most frequently hunted small cat in South America.

FLAT-HEADED CAT
This is a rare and elusive cat from India and parts of Southeast Asia. It has reddish-brown fur tipped with white, which gives it a silvery appearance. Little is known about its behavior, but it appears to live along riverbanks, probably catching fish, frogs, and birds, as well as small mammals.

Spots at the base of the tail become rings at the tip

Ocelot

Geoffroy's cat

The white ear spots are used to signal to other cats

GEOFFROY'S CAT
Geoffroy's cat (called after its discoverer, Etienne Geoffroy St. Hilaire, a 19th-century French naturalist) lives in forests and jungles from South American Bolivia to Patagonia. It can live at high altitudes and in Argentina is known as the mountain cat. It swims and climbs well and often sleeps in trees during the daylight hours.

The dark spots are similar to but smaller than those of the ocelot

The claws, hidden by soft pads, are sharpened by climbing

CUTTING BACK
If deforestation (destruction of the forests and jungles for development) continues at the present rate, the delicate balance of nature will be overturned forever and the beautiful cats that live in the forests will soon become extinct.

Speed king

THE CHEETAH IS THE FASTEST LAND MAMMAL in the world. It has a short head and a beautiful fur coat like other cats, but in some ways it hardly seems like a true cat. Unlike other cats, which are all leaping cats (p. 11), the cheetah can be called a running cat because it has evolved to hunt fast-running animals, such as the gazelle, in open country. For this reason it is placed in a different group from all other cats and given a different Latin name, *Acinonyx jubatus*. The cheetah selects its prey by stalking in the usual way, but then, at very high speed, it will chase after the gazelle or antelope and kill it with a sharp bite to the neck. It will also eat hares and guinea fowl, and sometimes even ostriches. Female cheetahs live alone and guard their territories, only allowing visiting males to come near when they are in heat (pp. 24–25). Unlike the solitary females, male cheetahs sometimes live together in a small group, but only the dominant male will mate with a female. The male group will not allow any other males into their territory and have been known to kill intruders.

Small head with short, rounded ears

FAST FORWARD
The long legs and flexible backbone of the cheetah enable it to run at up to 70 mph (110 kmh), faster than any other land mammal. It can reach its maximum speed in three seconds, from a standing start.

NO CONTEST
The acceleration of a cheetah is comparable to that of this powerful Ferrari, but the animal can only keep up its speed for about 550 ft (170 m).

Long, slender legs

Narrow, doglike paws

GET A GRIP
Like the dog, the cheetah extends its claws while it is running, to help it get a good grip on the ground. The claws are fairly blunt, only slightly curved, and very strong.

WANDERING WAYS
The mother cheetah usually gives birth to between one and eight cubs, which she keeps hidden in the long grass while they are very young. She does not have a permanent den but moves her cubs around every few days.

Supple, muscular back

Powerful hindquarters

INDIAN TAKE-OUT
In the past, cheetahs were often caught and trained to help huntsmen kill antelope and gazelle. Indian miniatures, painted to record the reign of the Mogul emperor Akbar in the 16th century, show the cheetahs' role. They were sent after prey, and having knocked it down would wait for their masters to complete the kill and take the carcass away.

CHEETAH
Cheetahs are becoming very rare. In wildlife parks their daytime activities are frequently disturbed by tourists, and although protected by law, they are still killed by poachers for their fur. Cheetahs used to be found in India and throughout Africa, but today the main population lives in Namibia and Zimbabwe (southern Africa). The cheetah hunts by day and usually drags its kill into bushes so that it cannot be driven away from its meal by vultures and other carnivores.

The striped tail is more than half the length of the head and body

ALL FURRED UP
The fur on the neck and shoulders is thicker than elsewhere. It forms a sort of "mane," which is hardly visible in adults but shows clearly, as in this Victorian engraving, in cubs and young animals.

MERGER
The king cheetah of southern Africa is very rare and was once classed as a separate species. The spots on its coat join to form stripes on its back.

Cats' kin

Broader head and longer face than a domestic cat's

THE MANY DIFFERENT BREEDS of domestic cat that are found in the world today, from Europe to Japan, are all descended from one wild species called *Felis silvestris*, the wildcat. This small cat is a widespread and highly adaptable species, which explains why it lives so easily and comfortably near humans. The wildcat is found in the forests of Europe, the rocky lands of western Asia and India, and the grasslands of Africa, and differs slightly in each habitat. In northern Europe, the Scottish wildcat (*Felis silvestris grampia*) has a stocky body and thick fur, to cope with life in cold climates. In Africa, where the climate is hot, the cat (*Felis silvestris lybica*) has a finer body, longer legs, and short hair. In India, the wildcat or Indian desert cat (*Felis silvestris ornata*) lives in hot, dry country, and is usually spotted. The wildcat shows many slight color variations, and the female is usually paler than the male. The wildcat from Africa is the most likely ancestor of the domestic cat, which was called *Felis catus* by Linnaeus (pp. 10–11).

WILD IN THE HIGHLANDS
The Scottish wildcat is still found in small numbers in the forests of Scotland, but it is in danger of extinction because it interbreeds with domestic cats that are living wild (feral cats, see pp. 60–61). This cat is like a large, heavily built tabby, but it is much fiercer.

Scottish wildcat

Shortish tail with blunt end

WEE WILDCATS
Kittens usually go out hunting with their mother at about 12 weeks and are independent at about five months. Although kittens of the African wildcat can become good pets, Scottish wildcat kittens have proved difficult to tame.

OUT OF AFRICA
African wildcats live all over Africa in many different habitats, from deserts to woodlands. When mating, they caterwaul like domestic cats and also meow harshly. They are not as shy as northern wildcats and often live close to villages and farms, interbreeding with domestic cats.

NOT CHOOSY
The Indian desert cat will interbreed with the northern wildcat, the African wildcat, and the domestic cat, so it certainly could have played a part in the ancestry of the domestic cat. It has a long, black-tipped tail, and the soles of its feet are black. It lives in hot, dry places and hunts small animals such as mice and lizards.

Ragged ears probably indicate many battles

WHO HAS TAMED WHOM?
The domestic tabby is not very different from its wild ancestor in its looks and behavior. Indeed, it has been said that the cat has tamed people and not the other way around (pp. 26–27).

Close relatives
The civet and the genet are not true cats but are sometimes mistaken for them and behave like them. They are carnivores and belong to the mongoose family, which also includes the rare linsangs and the meerkat. Although their heads are similar to those of cats, their skulls are different.

GENET
Although this little animal has a long, very un-catlike tail, its head looks similar to a cat's.

CIVET
The civet and the genet are forest dwellers and hunt and feed at night. Their bodies are patterned with spots or stripes.

Indian desert (or wild) cat

45

The taming of the cat

CATS PROBABLY BEGAN LIVING NEAR HUMAN SETTLEMENTS because it was easy to catch the rats and mice that were feeding on stored grain. People soon saw how useful cats were at destroying these pests, so they were encouraged to remain. Any kittens born nearby would have been tamed, and soon the cat was part of the household. Nobody knows when cats first started living with people, but it was probably at least 5,000 years ago. At the height of the great Egyptian civilization 3,000 years ago, the cat was already a common domestic animal, and it appears in many Egyptian tomb paintings. Eventually, the cat became one of the most sacred animals in Egypt. It is, therefore, probable that the cat was first domesticated by the ancient Egyptians, and that the wildcat of North Africa is the most likely ancestor of all domestic cats (pp. 44–45). However, it is also possible that the cat was tamed at about the same time in many different countries of Europe and Asia, wherever the wildcat lived. Today, there are domestic cats in every part of the world where there are humans.

MUMMIFIED MOUSER
When one of the sacred cats of ancient Egypt died, its body was mummified (treated to prevent decay), wrapped in cloths, and placed in a special tomb. When archeologists began to excavate these tombs during the last century, they found millions of mummified cats piled on top of each other.

PERSIAN PUSS
The fluffy, longhaired cats from Persia (now Iran) belong to one of the oldest breeds of domestic cat, although this ancient, hollow earthenware model from the 13th-century looks more like a spotted cat than a long-haired breed (pp. 56–57). Most longhaired pedigree cats throughout the world today are descended from cats brought from Turkey and Iran in the 18th and 19th centuries.

Egyptian mau

ANCIENT IMAGE
The spotted Egyptian mau is a domestic cat originating in Egypt. The word mau means "cat." Although this is a new breed which first appeared in Europe in the 1950s, its graceful, lithe body and green eyes, and the pale background color of the coat, make it more like the cats of ancient Egypt than perhaps any other cat, with the possible exception of the Abyssinian (pp. 52–53).

POMPEIAN PET
After the eruption of Mount Vesuvius (Italy) in A.D. 79, Pompeii and Herculaneum were destroyed, but the lava that covered the cities preserved a lot of evidence of the life there. This mosaic of a cat carrying off a bird was found in almost perfect condition.

FIGHTING LIKE CAT AND DOG
Two Greek men appear to be encouraging their animals to fight. It is interesting to see that both the cat and the dog are on leads. The way the dog is standing, with its front legs down and its nose pushed forward, shows that it doesn't really want to fight. It just wants to tease the cat, which is arching its back and ready to attack.

CATCHER CAT
A wall painting in the tomb of an Egyptian sculptor, Nebamun (around 1400 B.C.), is a scene of the dead man catching wildfowl in the Nile delta. This detail shows his cat holding two birds in its claws and one in its mouth, helping its owner by retrieving the birds.

CAT ON A PEDESTAL
Cat adoration in Egypt reached a peak with worship of the cat goddess Bastet, usually shown as a woman with a cat's head. She often carried a sistrum (a musical instrument) and an aegis (a shield) decorated with a lioness's head. She was associated with happiness and warmth, and loved people dancing and having a good time.

Because cats were considered sacred, they were often used to decorate jewelry, like this Egyptian gold and carnelian ring

SLAYING THE SERPENT
In this illustration from the Egyptian *Book of the Dead*, the sun god Ra, in the form of a cat, slays Apep, the serpent of darkness.

Myths and legends

MOSCOW MOUSER
Cats play a prominent part in Russian fairy tales.

FOR THE LAST 3,000 YEARS, since they were first revered as sacred animals by the ancient Egyptians, cats have played a major role in the folklore of many countries around the world. This may be because cats are such puzzling creatures. In the daytime they are often soft, sleepy, and affectionate, but at night they turn into silent and efficient hunters. In many European countries, huge numbers of cats were cruelly killed during the late Middle Ages, because they were thought to be associated with witchcraft. On the whole, they had a much better time in eastern countries such as Myanmar (Burma), where magical powers were thought to be for the good. At sea, too, cats enjoyed a good reputation, not only because they killed rats on board ship, but also because many sailors believed that cats could forecast storms.

HAUNTING TALE
In Japan, myth has it that cats have the power to turn into super-spirits when they die. This may be because, according to the Buddhist religion, the body of the cat is the temporary resting place of the soul of very spiritual people.

BLESSED BIRMAN
The Birman is the sacred cat of Myanmar (formerly Burma). According to legend, a Burmese temple was attacked and the high priest killed. His favorite white temple cat jumped onto his head and was transformed into a Birman. Where the paws touched the priest, the fur remained white, a symbol of goodness. This miracle encouraged the remaining priests to repel the invaders.

CAT CHARIOT
During the early Renaissance period in Europe, the cat was widely persecuted. This was perhaps because of a revival of interest in the Norse love goddess Freya, whose chariot was drawn by cats. This revival spurred the Christian church to attempt to purge Europe of the symbols of paganism.

FAMILIAR CATS
From about 1400 to 1700, the cat was thought of as a witch's "familiar"— her private connection with the devil. Witches were also thought to be able to turn themselves into cats at will. Many cats were therefore persecuted, and there were mass burnings in many parts of Europe, most notably in the French town of Metz.

BOND CAT
Ernst Blofeld, the arch-enemy of 007 spy James Bond, always had a white Persian cat at his side when confronting Bond.

British black shorthair

PUSS IN BOOTS
In southern France, there was once a wide belief in *matagots,* or magician cats. One of the most famous of these was Puss in Boots, created by Charles Perrault. This cat was so crafty that it won for its master a fortune and a princess for a wife.

BLACK MAGIC
Belief as to whether a black cat brings good or bad luck has varied over the centuries and from country to country. In Britain, a black cat crossing your path brings good luck, while in the American Midwest, it is good luck if a black cat visits your house, but bad luck if it stays.

Aristocats

IN THE MID-19TH CENTURY it became fashionable to own exotic cats, and clubs were formed to determine standards and compare types. During the 20th century, many breeds have been developed that look very different from the cat's wild ancestors, and it is sometimes difficult to remember that inside every champion is a wild animal with the instincts of a hunter. But the basic behavioral patterns of cats do not change, although they may appear to do so. Sometimes, this apparent change in behavior may be because the kittens of pedigree cats are often reared in a cattery in large numbers, for sale, and not individually in a human home. If a cat is to be an affectionate companion, it must be handled and talked to starting as soon after birth as possible. If it is brought up without this sort of human contact, and then taken from its mother at six weeks old to be placed with a family, it may seem nervous and disturbed. This nervousness is often blamed on the cat's highly bred temperament, but it might be caused by a lack of social contact from birth, and by being removed from its mother too soon.

FIRST SHOW
Harrison Weir, who staged the world's first modern cat show in London in 1871, is seen with the winner, a Persian kitten.

SHOW OFF
It is argued that the showing of pedigree cats has helped to create the great variety of breeds in the world today, although many people find the genetic experimentation necessary to develop new breeds distasteful.

FIT AND FLUFFED-UP
Grooming longhaired cats (pp. 56–57) is necessary to prevent tangling and get rid of excess hair. It is particularly important before a cat show, when a cat should look fluffed-up and in peak condition.

ORANGES
Red self longhairs were originally known, for obvious reasons, as oranges. This is a fairly rare breed, but they were known in Britain as long ago as 1895. The beautiful red coat should show no shading or tabby markings.

Deep orange coat

Thickset body

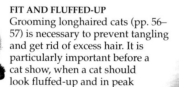

Ears are sometimes
almost transparent

Body is muscular
but elegant

The Russian blue has a very
"aristocratic" profile. The
nose is wedge-shaped and
the ears are large and
slightly pointed.

Russian blue

Wide-set, almost
turquoise eyes

BLUE BEAUTY
The Russian blue has had a
great many names in its
history, including Spanish cat
and Maltese cat, but it is
generally thought to be a
Russian breed. The breed
was exported to Britain in
the 16th century. One of
the most famous was
Vashka, the
beloved pet of
Nicholas I, czar
(ruler) of Russia.

Long, fine -
boned legs
with small,
oval paws

Thick, plush double
coat stands out from
the cat's body because
of its density

Long, tapering
tail

Powerful hind legs

Large, round,
copper-colored
eyes

Red self longhair

Small,
rounded ears

UNLUCKY 13
In 1898, a party of 13 dined at London's famous
Savoy Hotel. The first guest to leave was killed
soon after, fulfilling an old superstition. In the
1920s, sculptor Basil Ionides was commissioned
to carve a wooden cat about 3 ft (1 m) high.
At the Savoy today, Kaspar the cat always
sits at the table when there are 13 diners,
and is served the whole meal.

The red self
has a very
different profile
from the
Russian blue.
The nose is so
flat that the
animal sometimes
has trouble
breathing
through it.

Short, solid legs

51

Shorthairs

Most cats had short hair until about 100 years ago, when it became fashionable to own cats and experiment with breeding (pp. 50–51). A cat with a short coat could survive and fend for itself more easily. There was no danger of the cat's becoming tangled in branches or being grabbed by enemies, and less chance of a skin disease as a result of matted fur. Even today, the shorthaired breeds are more robust. Pedigree shorthaired cats fall into three main categories: the British shorthair, the American shorthair, and the foreign or Oriental shorthair. The British shorthair is a stocky, muscular cat with shortish legs. The American shorthair developed from ancestors of the British shorthairs that were taken to the United States by early settlers. It is larger and more lithe than the British type and has slightly longer legs. Among the most popular cats today are the Oriental shorthairs. They are sleeker than the other shorthairs, with smaller heads and longer legs. The Siamese and Abyssinian are two well-known breeds. There are many non-pedigree shorthaired cats, of all shapes and sizes, which can be as beautiful as their purebred cousins.

American portraits, like this one by Ammi Phillips (1788–1865), often included the family pet

Large, pointed ears set far apart

Almond-shaped green eyes

Small, oval-shaped paws with black pads

Longish tail tipped with black

SEW MUCH FUN
In the early part of the century, cutely painted kittens, like the two here, were often used to illustrate birthday cards and postcards. Thread spools are still favorite playthings for kittens.

ABYSSINIAN *left*
No one knows for sure where the Abyssinian was first bred, but it looks like the cats shown on ancient Egyptian tomb paintings. It comes in many colors including usual (brown), sorrel (light copper), blue, fawn, lilac (pinkish-gray), and silver. It is a beautiful and very graceful cat.

*Large ears set
high on the head*

*Heart-shaped face
with very round,
bright green eyes*

*Tortoiseshell-and-
white coat covers
thickset body*

TORTOISESHELL-AND-WHITE
These pretty cats, with their distinctive coats, are very familiar
but hard to breed. To produce a tortoiseshell, females are best
mated to a solid-colored black, red, or cream male, but even then
there may be only one kitten with the desired coloring.
Tortoiseshells are almost always female. They are usually lively
cats and make charming family pets.

*Fur separates
when the back
is bent*

LOOKOUT
Like all cats, this tabby likes to
know what's going on and has
selected a good perch. Non-
pedigree cats are sometimes less
nervous than highly bred cats
(pp. 50–51) and usually make
good pets.

*Small, oval
paws with blue
to lavender-
colored pads*

KORAT *above*
The Korat is one of the oldest breeds
of cat. It comes originally from
Thailand and is thought to bring
good luck to its owner. The breed was
first taken to the United States in the
1950s and arrived in Britain in the
1970s. It is a gentle, rather nervous
cat with a heart-shaped head and
a dusky blue coat.

BURMESE *right*
Like the Abyssinian, the Burmese
comes in a variety of coat colors, of
which brown is the original and, to
some, ideal color. Brown cats similar
to today's Burmese were recorded as
living in Buddhist temples in Myanmar
as long ago as the 15th century. The
Burmese is an affectionate, intelligent
cat that hates to be left alone.

Continued on next page

MR. AND MRS. CLARK AND PERCY
There is no doubt that artists like to paint cats. From the 1400s to the present day, cats have appeared in great works of art. In this famous painting by British artist David Hockney (born 1937) of his friends Ossie Clark and his ex-wife, their large white cat, Percy, is almost the center of the painting.

HOPE SPRINGS ETERNAL
This cat can smell the scent of the bird that was in the cage.

Ginger and white cat

MR. MISTOFFELEES
Old Possum's Book of Practical Cats by the poet T. S. Eliot describes wonderful cats, full of character. Mr. Mistoffelees (like all black cats; p. 49) has his own share of magic. Indeed, Eliot describes him as "The Original Conjuring Cat."

Ringed, fluffy tail

MISS ZOE DE BELLECOURT
This very proper 18th-century girl was painted by the Scottish artist George Watson (1767–1837). Cats were considered suitable pets for young ladies at this time.

COLOR CHANGE
Because of the popularity of the Russian blue (above), attempts have been made to produce all-black and all-white versions of it. For some reason, Russian blues are most popular in New Zealand.

BEATEN BY A HEAD
This unusual piece of American folk art shows a cat head with a bird in its mouth. It was perhaps painted as a tribute to a good hunting cat (cats played an important part in early American homesteads), or it may have been someone's family emblem.

SIAMESE *below*
The first Siamese to arrive in Britain in the 1880s are believed to have been a gift to the British embassy from the Court of Siam (modern Thailand). The Siamese is a highly intelligent, noisy cat, and often will not tolerate rivals for its owner's affections.

Thin, tapering tail

Long, pointed ears

Tabby cat

Fluffy coat in excellent condition

Bright eyes are a sign of good health

TWO'S COMPANY
More non-pedigree cats have tabby coats than any other kind of markings. Non-pedigree cats are often more robust than highly bred cats, because inbreeding (breeding within a closely related group) can cause physical weaknesses. These two cats clearly get along. They display no aggressive signs toward each other.

Long, slim legs

Small, neat paws

Longhairs

ALL WILD CATS HAVE A TWO-LAYER FUR COAT (pp. 14–15), and in cold countries, all mammals, including cats, tend to have thicker and longer fur than those from hot countries. But no wild cat has the luxurious fur of the longhaired domestic cat (although the Pallas cat comes close). Long hair would be a disadvantage to a wild cat because it would become matted and tangled in bushes (pp. 52–53). However, because longhaired cats are very attractive, this characteristic was specially selected by cat breeders in the past and is now common. The Persian is probably the oldest breed of longhaired cat, and most longhairs are of the Persian type. The breed may have been brought into Europe from western Asia on several occasions over the last few hundred years. Another very old breed is the Angora, which came from Turkey. Longhaired cats are usually placid by nature and make excellent companions, but they do need more attention than shorthaired cats.

BIRMAN
The Birman has a longer body than a typical longhair, and markings similar to a Siamese. Although legend has it that the breed evolved from a white temple cat (pp. 48–49), it may, in fact, be a cross between a Siamese and a Persian. It always has white feet.

ANGORA
This early engraving shows an Angora, possibly the first longhair to be seen in Europe.

Large, round white paws

Neck ruff

Short head with long, pink-tipped nose

Long, feathery tail

TURKISH VANS
This cat is often referred to as the Turkish swimming cat, because it is said to be particularly fond of playing in water. It takes its name from the isolated area around Lake Van in southeast Turkey, where it has been bred for several hundred years.

Frowning expression caused by horizontal crease between the eyes

PALLAS'S CAT
This wild cat is named after Peter Simon Pallas (1741–1811), the German naturalist, who discovered it in the area around the Caspian Sea, in the Soviet Union. It has a long, thick coat, which helps to protect it from the harsh climate of its habitat. Pallas thought that it might be an ancestor of the longhaired domestic cats, although this is now not thought likely.

Blunt-ended, plumelike tail

RED SELF
Although this breed was shown in Britain at the end of the last century (pp. 50–51), all pedigree cat breeding dwindled during World Wars I and II, and the red self became rare in Britain and Europe. Recently, there has been a revival of interest in it, although there are few good examples of this cat.

MAINE COON
The Maine coon is the oldest American breed of cat and one of the largest. Tradition says that it roamed free in the state of Maine in its early history and was compared with the raccoon, which has similar markings and hunting habits – hence its name. In fact, it probably descends from American farm cats and longhaired cats brought back from Europe by sailors.

Strong legs, with large round paws

Color woodcut by American artist Elizabeth Norton (1887–1985)

Curious cats

THE BREEDING OF CATS for special characteristics, like different colored coats, extra big ears, a reduced tail, or very fluffy fur, was begun at the start of the 20th century (pp. 50–51). Since then, many different breeds have been developed. By selective breeding, almost any part of the cat can be altered. It is possible that these special features could appear as natural mutations in a wild cat, but the animal would probably die before passing on these abnormalities. With domestic cats, many kinds of features can be produced by inbreeding and selection, and offspring can be given very special care, so that the line will be carried on. Sometimes curiosities in the wild, like the white tiger, are perfectly healthy, as are some new domestic breeds like the Burmilla, a cross between a Burmese cat and a chinchilla cat. But all too often, excessive inbreeding produces an animal with serious health problems. Whether breeders should continue trying to develop new breeds is an open question.

CHESHIRE CAT
This stained glass window commemorates the British writer Lewis Carroll (1832–1898) who immortalized the perpetually grinning Cheshire Cat in *Alice's Adventures in Wonderland.*

THE SPHYNX
This cat's appearance is probably not everyone's idea of beauty. Hairless kittens are born from time to time as a natural genetic abnormality. One such kitten, born in 1966 to an ordinary black and white cat in Canada, was used as a founding sire (male cat used for fathering kittens) for a new breed of hairless cats.

DEVON REX
As a result of a mutation, which was selected for the founding of a new breed, the Devon and Cornish (originating from Devon and Cornwall in England) rex cats are unique in that every hair on their bodies is soft and curly. They are lively animals and make affectionate family cats.

The curly fur is short, soft, and close-lying with no guard hairs (pp. 14–15)

Devon rex

The head is wedge-shaped with a longish nose. The nose should be roughly the same color as the coat. The ears are large and slightly rounded, and the eyes are almond-shaped.

Even the whiskers are curly

THE OWL AND THE PUSSYCAT
A cat and bird friendship would be a very curious thing indeed. However, in Edward Lear's (1812–1888) famous poem, the owl and the pussycat fall in love, marry, and live happily ever after.

MIX 'N MATCH
In zoos and circuses, lions and tigers sometimes mate. When the father is a lion, the cubs are called ligers, and when the tiger is the father, they are called tigons. These animals, although healthy, are often unable to bear young. However, a female liger in Munich was successfully mated back to a lion and the cub was reared to adulthood.

Long, flexible tail

MANX
A kitten without a tail may be born in any litter, and the Manx has long been established as a breed. Manx means from the Isle of Man, off the northwest coast of England. Although not originally from the island, tailless cats became common there at least 200 years ago, probably as a result of its geographical isolation and the resulting inbreeding.

Well-defined patches of black, cream, orange, and white fur

Manx cats have no tail at all, like this one (a rumpy), a tiny bump (a riser), a movable tail stump (a stumpy or stubby), or a small tail (a longy)

Strong back legs

IN BLACK AND WHITE
The striking white tiger was once not uncommon in north and east central India, but there are few there now. The unusual color is the result of a dominance of white genes similar to those in white domestic cats.

NEATLY FOLDED
Ears that turn over or hang down are a common feature of domestic dogs but are rarely seen in cats, but the folded ear, like the absence of a tail, can occur as a natural mutation. A white kitten born in Scotland with folded ears in 1961 was used as a sire for a new breed called the Scottish fold.

Street life

A<small>LL CITIES HAVE A SECRET WORLD</small> of teeming animal life, where hunters and hunted co-exist successfully. Cats find plenty of pigeons, rats, mice, and cockroaches to prey upon in alleyways, drainpipes, and trash cans. City cats have their own territories. They crawl into basements, under sheds and warehouses, or up onto roofs. Male cats (toms) mark and defend their territories in the same way that house cats and wild cats do. Territory size is roughly linked to an animal's size and needs. Domestic cats that can scavenge food scraps or are fed by humans can live in much greater density than wild cats in competition for prey. Females (queens) also have territories, and will find hidden places to have their kittens. Cats are useful in cities because they clear away some garbage and reduce the number of rats and mice. When well-meaning people feed urban cats, they can become too numerous, which upsets the balance of the concrete jungle. In some cities, cats are caught, neutered, and released so they can keep on catching rats and mice but not breed again.

Illustration from *The Historie of Foure-footed Beastes* by Edward Topsell, 1607

CATS ON A HOT TIN ROOF
Their roaming nature often means that cats take to the rooftops. This territory gives them independence from human interference and sometimes allows them access to interesting places. This delightful scene by French artist and engraver Grandville (1803–1847), is entitled *"The Heartaches of an English Cat."*

Tabby markings form the basic feline coat pattern

The coat is slightly matted, a sign that this cat is not in peak condition

TABBY TEMPERAMENT
It may seem strange, but a cat's color and the markings of its coat seem to be associated with its temperament. Cats that live in cities have to be calm and cunning by nature, and blotched tabby cats and black and white cats seem to have temperaments best suited to city life.

STREET FIGHTERS
There are 58 million cats in the United States. It is not easy to tell the difference between cats that live with people and go out into the streets at night, and those that live like wild animals, away from human contact all the time. Street or alley cats are usually more wary of humans than house cats that go out at night, and tend to look scruffier. They run away when approached, and may be ragged-eared and scarred from frequent battles.

The ear is ragged and scarred, a certain sign of battles fought

The eye is damaged, the result of either a fight or an inadequate diet

TOM, DICK, OR HARRY?
When a female cat is in heat (pp. 24–25), several males in succession may mate with her. This means the kittens might not have the same father and might look different from each other, as in the painting above. Indeed, one female is known to have given birth to a very mixed litter of non-pedigree cats and one perfect Siamese.

Feral cats

Feral refers to domestic animals that once lived under human control but have returned to live and breed in the wild. Feral cats are often found on islands where they were left by sailors, but where there are now few humans. These cats can do serious damage to local wildlife.

ONLY A WHISKER
There is a fine line between a street or alley cat and a feral cat. Indeed, some people claim that they are one and the same. Certainly, some alley cats can live totally outside human control, but most do depend indirectly on human life.

CATASTROPHE
This Parisian group is protesting against a proposed plan to destroy the feral cat populations living in Paris. The objectors believed that such a move would be a disaster, and upset the natural ecological balance, not only in Paris, but eventually in all France.

Caring for your cat

CATS ARE INDIVIDUAL ANIMALS with their own needs. Owning a cat means that you should provide it with regular, well-balanced meals, a warm bed, and a great deal of care and attention. If possible, every cat should be allowed outside to explore and establish its territory and to eat blades of grass, which help its digestion. Cat flaps in doors allow maximum freedom to cats and minimum annoyance to owners, but there may be the odd unwelcome visiting cat. Most people like to have their cat neutered unless they are intending to breed it. Your vet can tell you the correct age for neutering. It is also wise to have your cat vaccinated against feline enteritis and cat flu, both of which can be fatal. Kittens are irresistible, but before getting one, you should remember that a cat can live for over 20 years and will need constant care for all of that time – but the rewards will be great.

Kittens often appeared on the first Christmas cards made in the 19th-century

KAT KIT
All cats, especially the longhaired breeds, should be brushed regularly, otherwise they swallow a lot of hair when they lick their coats. The hair collects in the stomach as a fur ball, which can make the cat ill.

Water bowl

SCRATCH CLEAN
Every cat needs to clean its claws and stretch its body (pp. 26–27). A scratching post or an old piece of wood are ideal for this.

Food bowl

MOUSER MENU
Cats are carnivores and need to eat meat or fish daily. Hard bones that do not splinter are also a good idea as they help to keep the teeth and jaws clean and healthy. Water should always be available and is essential if dried food is part of the diet. Although cats like milk, it often causes stomach upset.

Scoop

Cat litter

Litter box

CREATURE COMFORTS
The cat is a territorial animal and needs its own sleeping place. However, it will often take over an armchair or bed, probably because these places smell reassuring rather than because they are especially comfortable.

DIGGING IN
Nearly all cats can be trained to use a litter box. The cat carefully buries its excreta, but the box needs to be cleaned out daily and the litter replaced often.

PLAYTIME
Cats love to play, and the exercise is good for them. A wad of paper is often enough to distract them. No toy should have a loose string that could wind around the animal's body or strangle it.

COLLARED
Many people think that a cat should not wear a collar because it might get caught on a twig or a tree branch. However, collars with an elastic strip in them allow the cat to escape in an emergency. It is advisable to attach an identification tag to the collar.

Front grill can be securely fastened

ON THE ROAD
Cats hate to be taken away from their own territory. They are extremely alert, and most cats know when their owners are about to go on vacation. It is often better to leave them in their own home and have somone come to feed them, than to take them with you or put them in a kennel. However, if this is not possible, a secure cat carrier, lined with a favorite blanket, is important. It should be brought out well in advance of any trip, even for a short visit, such as to the local vet, so that the animal can get used to it being around.

BASKET CASE
Few cats will sleep in a specially provided basket if it does not smell right. Cats like something that smells of their owner. So a cat basket should first be lined with newspaper, to help prevent drafts, and then covered with an old sweatshirt or other article of clothing. All places where the cat sleeps should be kept free from fleas by regular spraying or washing with an insecticide that will not harm the animal.

ALL YOU NEED IS LOVE
A cat needs not only clean food and a warm bed, but also affection as well. In return, it will display love for its owner. Cat ownership has been shown to benefit humans, particularly the elderly and those alone. The cat provides companionship, and stroking and petting it helps to release frustration and tension.

Index

A

Abyssinian, 17, 25, 46, 52-3
Acinonyx jubatus, 42
Africa, 6, 10, 11, 28, 32, 38-9, 43-4
African lion, 28-9
African wildcat, 39, 44-5
Amazon, 34-5, 37
American shorthair, 52
anal glands, 14, 21
Angora, 56
Argentina, 40-1
Arizona, 40
Asia, 10-1, 19, 28, 32-3, 36, 38-9, 40, 44, 46, 56
Audubon, John James, 36
Australia, 10
Aztecs, 35

B

balance, 18-9
Bangladesh, 31
behavior, 26-7, 50
big cats, 11, 18, 20, 23
Birman, 48, 56
black-footed cat, 10, 39
black leopard *see* panther
Blake, William, 30
bobcat, 10, 13, 24, 36
Bolivia, 41
brain, 13, 14-5, 25
Britain, 6, 8, 36, 49, 50-1, 53, 55, 57, 61
British National Cat Club, 50
British shorthair, 49, 52
Burma *see* Myanmar
Burmese, 53, 58
Burmilla, 58

C

camouflage, 6, 14, 30, 32, 36, 40
Canada, 36, 58
canine teeth, 8, 9, 12-3, 28
caracal, 38
care, 50, 62-3
carnassial teeth, 12-3

Carnivora, 10
carnivores, 6, 8, 10, 18, 43, 45, 62
Carroll, Lewis, 58
Caspian Sea, 57
cheetah, 7, 10-1, 15, 23, 32, 42-3
China, 30, 40
chinchilla, 58
civet, 45
claws, 7, 11, 12, 15, 20, 27, 41-2
clouded leopard, 10-1
Cocteau, Jean, 56
Colorado, 37
communication, 20, 26, 29, 32
Cornish rex, 58
cougar, 10, 36
cubs, 18, 24-5, 32, 43

D

Daniel, 29
desert lynx, 38
Devon rex, 58
Dinictis, 9
domestication, 46, 58

E

Egypt, 46-7
Egyptian mau, 46
Egyptians, 48, 52
Eliot, T. S., 54
Elizabeth I, 16
England, 31, 59
Eocene, 8
Europe, 10, 28, 36, 44, 46, 49, 56-7
evolution, 8, 26
extinction, 8, 11, 30, 34, 40-1, 44

F

Felidae, 6, 40
Felis catus, 10, 44
Felis leo, 10
Felis silvestris, 10, 44, 46
feral cats, 44, 61
fishing cat, 23
flat-headed cat, 40
Florence, 32

fossil cats, 8, 9, 11
France, 49, 61
fur trade, 14, 32, 36, 38, 40, 43

G

Ganges, 30
Ganku, Kishi, 31
genet, 45
Geoffroy's cat, 41
Germany, 9
gestation, 24
ginger cat, 54
Gir Forest, 28
Gozzoli, 32
Grandville, 60
Greenland, 6
grooming, 20-1

H

hairless cat, 58
hearing, 14-5, 16-7
Herculaneum, 46
Hercules, 29
Hiroshige, Ando, 21
Hockney, David, 54
Hoplophoneus, 9
hunting, 7, 11-2, 18, 22-3, 24, 26, 28, 32, 55

I

Incas, 34
incisor teeth, 13
India, 11, 23, 28, 30-1, 38, 40, 43, 44, 59
Indian desert cat, 45
Iones, Basil, 51
Iran (Persia), 38, 46
Isle of Man, 13, 59

J

Jacobson's organ, 14, 16
jaguar, 6, 10, 14, 33, 34-5
Japan, 7, 21, 24, 31, 44, 48

K L

Kipling, Rudyard, 7, 33
Landseer, Sir Edwin, 8
Lear, Edward, 58
leopard, 10-1, 14, 18, 22, 24, 32-3
leopard cat, 40
liger, 59
Lindisfarne Gospels, 6
Linnaeus, 10, 44
lion, 8, 10-1, 13, 14-5, 25, 27, 28-9, 30, 32, 40, 59
London, 8, 16, 31, 50-1
longhaired cats, 50, 56-7, 62
Los Angeles, 8
Lucca, Duke of, 32
lynx, 10, 36-7, 38

M

Maine coon, 57
Maltese cat, 51
man-eaters, 31
Manx cats, 13, 59
margay, 40
mating, 24, 42, 61
Metz, 49
Mexico, 35, 40
Miacis, 9
Mochica culture, 37
Mount Vesuvius, 46
Mogul empire, 31, 43
Muybridge, Eadweard, 19
Myanmar (Burma), 48, 53

N O

Namibia, 43
Nebamun, 47
Nebuchadnezzar, 29
Nelson's column, 8
New Zealand, 55
Nicholas I, Czar, 51
Nigeria, 33
Nile, 47
Norton, Elizabeth, 57
North Africa, 46
North America, 9, 10, 36
ocelot, 14, 40
Old Testament, 29
Oligocene, 9
orange cat, 50
Oriental shorthair, 52

P

Pallas, Peter Simon, 57
Pallas's cat, 56-7
panther, 14, 22-3, 33
Paris, 61
Patagonia, 34, 41
pedigree cats, 50, 57
Perrault, Charles, 49
Persia *see* Iran
Persian cat, 13, 46, 49, 50, 56
Peru, 34, 35, 37
Pompeii, 46
pride, 6, 7, 18, 21, 22, 24, 26, 28
puma, 10, 25, 36-7
purring, 12, 15

R

Ra, 47
Rancho la Brea, 8
red self, 50-1, 57
Renaissance, 29, 32, 49
rex, 14; *see also* Cornish rex and Devon rex
Rousseau, Henri, 30
Russian blue, 51, 55

S

saber-toothed cat, 8, 9
Sahara, 39
St. Hilaire, Geoffroy, 41
sand cat, 39
scent, 14, 17, 22, 25, 26
scent glands, 20-1, 27
Scotland, 44, 59
Scottish fold, 59
Scottish wildcat, 44
selective breeding, 58
senses, 10, 15, 16-7, 18
serval, 14, 23, 38-9
shorthairs, 49, 52-5
Siam *see* Thailand
Siamese, 25, 52, 55, 56, 61
Siberia, 11, 30
Siberian tiger, 6, 30
sight, 17
skeleton, 6, 12-3, 15
small cats, 10, 12, 16, 18, 20, 22-3
Smilodon, 8,9
snow leopard, 10, 12, 33
sorrel Abyssinian, 17, 25, 52
South America, 8, 10, 34-5, 36-7, 40-1
South Dakota, 9
Southampton, Earl of, 16
Southeast Asia, 30, 33, 40
Soviet Union, 57
Spanish cat, 51
Sundarbans forest, 31

T

tabby cat, 6, 10, 26, 44-5, 53, 55, 60
tapetum lucidum, 16
taste, 17
taste-smell, 14, 16
teeth, 8, 9, 10, 12-3, 23, 28
territories, 20, 26-7, 28, 30-1, 32, 34, 37, 42, 60, 62
Thailand (Siam), 53, 55
Thylacosmilus, 8
tiger, 10-1, 12-3, 14, 18-9, 24, 30-1, 32, 58-9
tigon, 59
tongue, 14, 17, 20
Topsell, Edward, 60
tortoiseshell, 16, 27, 53
touch, 14, 17, 20
Tower of London, 16
Turkey, 46, 56
Turkish Van, 56

U W Z

urban cats, 60
U.S., 34, 37, 49, 52, 53, 57, 61
Wain, Louis, 50
Watson, George, 54
Weir, Harrison, 50
whiskers, 6, 15, 16-7
white tiger, 58-9
wildcat, 10, 39, 44-5, 46
witchcraft, 48-9
Zimbabwe, 43

Acknowledgments

Dorling Kindersley would like to thank:

Trevor Smith and all the staff at Trevor Smith's Animal World.
Jim Clubb of Clubb-Chipperfield.
Nicki Barrass of A1 Animals.
Terry Moore of the Cat Survival Trust.
The staff of the British Museum and the Natural History Museum for their assistance.
Jacquie Gulliver and Lynne Williams for their work on the initial stages of the book.
Christian Sévigny and Liz Sephton for design assistance.
Claire Gillard and Céline Carez for editorial assistance.

Picture credits

t=top b=bottom l=left r=right c=center

Animals Unlimited: 53b; Ardea: R.Beames 40c; K. Fink 40tr; Bridgeman Art Library: back jacket bl above, 28tc, 62tl; Bibliothèque Nationale, Paris 28tb; Chadwick Gallery, Warwicks 52c; National Gallery, London 30tl detail; National Gallery of Scotland 54bl; Victoria & Albert Museum, London 20tl; Courtesy of the Trustees of the British Museum: 6tr, 22bl, 31tr; In the Collection of the Duke of Buccleuch & Queensberry KT: 16cr detail; Jean Loup Charmet: 7tr; Bruce Coleman Ltd: 57tr; Jen & Des Bartlett 13c, 23bl, 25c, 28c; Jane Burton 16cb; Jane Burton & Kim Taylor 16cl; Eric Creighton 26cl; Gerald Cubitt 39br, 43b; G. D. Plage 24cl; Hans Reinhard 12c, 16tl, 24bl, 37tc, 42-43; Norman Tomalin 45bl; Konrad Wothe 22br; Rod Williams 11c, 33cb; Gunter Ziesler 42c, 43tl; E.T.

Archive: 24tr, 62br; © Sheila Roberts 1971, 63tc; Mary Evans Picture Library: 10cl, 19t, 27cr, 49tl, tr, 58br; Werner Forman Archive: 33b, 35tr; Freer Gallery of Art, Washington: 21tl detail, Acc. No. 04.357; Robert Harding Picture Library: 49bl; Marc Henrie 50cl; "Mr & Mrs Clark & Percy" 1970-1, © David Hockney/photo Tate Gallery: 54tl; Michael Holford: front jacket tr & tl below, 31tl, c, 35b, 37c, 47tr, 47br, 48cl; Hulton-Deutsch Collection: 30b; Hutchison Library: 34c; Image Bank: 54c; Images Colour Library: 47bl, 48tl, 58tl; Kobal Collection: 11cl, 22t, 49cr; M.R. Long: 9c; LYNX: 36tr; Mansell Collection: 13bl; Metropolitan Museum of Art: 57b; Museum of American Folk Art: 52t; National Gallery of Art, Washington: 55tr (gift of Edgar William & Bernice Chrysler Garbisch); Natural History Museum: 8tl, bl, 12bl, 13tl, br, 33c, 35c, 36cr, 37tc, 38c; Natural History Photographic Agency: Agence Nature 18bl; Anthony Bannister 42b; Nigel

Dennis 45tl; Patrick Fagot 19c; Peter Johnson 14cl, 45cl; Stephen Krasman 16tr; Gérard Lacz 12tl, 58tr, 59bl; Northampton Historical Society, Mass.: 15tc; Oxford Scientific Films: 37tl, 39tl; Roy Coombes 27c; Sean Morris 41b; Richard Packwood 12cb; Kjell Sandved 59br; Bernard Schellhammer 53cr; Quadrant Picture Library: 42cb; Courtesy of The Savoy: 51cr; Scala: Palazzo Medici Riccardi, Florence 32bl detail; Museo Nationale, Napoli 46tl; National Museum, Athens 47tl; Spectrum Colour Library: 8br; Frank Spooner Pictures: 61br; Survival Anglia; Dieter & Mary Plage 32tl; Alan Root 27tr; Maurice Tibbles 14tr; Amoret Tanner: 28tl; Victoria & Albert Museum Picture Library: 43tr detail; Zefa: 16ct; E. & P. Bauer 23bl, 38bl; M. N. Boulton 11bl; Bramaz 63br; G. Dimijian 21cr; D. Kessel 35tl; Lummerc 20br; Orion 19cb

Illustrations by: Dan Wright

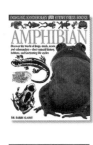
AMPHIBIAN

ANCIENT CHINA

ANCIENT EGYPT

ANCIENT GREECE

ANCIENT ROME

ARCHEOLOGY

ARCTIC & ANTARCTIC

ARMS & ARMOR

ASTRONOMY

AZTEC, INCA & MAYA

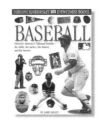
BASEBALL

BATTLE

BIBLE LANDS

BIRD

BOAT

BOOK

BUILDING

BUTTERFLY & MOTH

CAR

CASTLE

CAT

CHEMISTRY

COSTUME

COWBOY

CRIME & DETECTION

CRYSTAL & GEM

DANCE

DESERT

DINOSAUR

DOG

EAGLE & BIRDS OF PREY

EARLY HUMANS

EARTH

ECOLOGY

ELECTRICITY

ELECTRONICS

ELEPHANT

ENERGY

EPIDEMIC

EVEREST

EVOLUTION

EXPLORER

FARM

FILM

FISH

FLAG

FLYING MACHINE

FORCE & MOTION — FOSSIL

FUTURE — GORILLA, MONKEY & APE

HORSE